WOMEN
IN
HISTORY

Women of the Suffrage Movement

Lydia Bjornlund

LUCENT
BOOKS®

THOMSON
★
GALE

San Diego • Detroit • New York • San Francisco • Cleveland • New Haven, Conn. • Waterville, Maine • London • Munich

On cover: Suffragettes march in New York in 1917 with a banner
urging President Wilson to support woman suffrage.

© 2003 by Lucent Books. Lucent Books is an imprint of The Gale Group, Inc.,
a division of Thomson Learning, Inc.

Lucent Books® and Thomson Learning™ are trademarks used herein under license.

For more information, contact
Lucent Books
27500 Drake Rd.
Farmington Hills, MI 48331-3535
Or you can visit our Internet site at http://www.gale.com

LIBRARY OF CONGRESS CATALOGING-IN-PUBLICATION DATA

Bjornlund, Lydia D.
  Women of the suffrage movement / by Lydia Bjornlund.
    v. cm. — (Women in history series)
Includes bibliographical references and index.
Summary: Examines leaders of the suffrage movement, the role of African
American women in the movement, militant suffragists, and antisuffragists.
    ISBN 1-59018-173-5 (hardback : alk. paper)
  1. Women—Suffrage—United States—History. 2. Suffragists—United States—
History—Juvenile literature. 3. Suffragists—United States—Biography—Juvenile
literature. 4. African Americans—Suffrage—History—Juvenile literature.
[1. Women—Suffrage. 2. Suffragists. 3. Women's rights. 4. Women—Biography.
5. African Americans—Biography. 6. African Americans—Suffrage.] I. Title.
II. Series.
    JK1898 .B56 2003
    324.6'23'092273—dc21

                             2002005528

Printed in the United States of America

Contents

Foreword

The story of the past as told in traditional historical writings all too often leaves the impression that if men are not the only actors in the narrative, they are assuredly the main characters. With a few notable exceptions, males were the political, military, and economic leaders in virtually every culture throughout recorded time. Since traditional historical scholarship focuses on the public arenas of government, foreign relations, and commerce, the actions and ideas of men—or at least of powerful men—are naturally at the center of conventional accounts of the past.

In the last several decades, however, many historians have abandoned their predecessors' emphasis on "great men" to explore the past "from the bottom up," a phenomenon that has had important consequences for the study of women's history. These social historians, as they are known, focus on the day-to-day experiences of the "silent majority"—those people typically omitted from conventional scholarship because they held relatively little political or economic sway within their societies. In the new social history, members of ethnic and racial minorities, factory workers, peasants, slaves, children,

and women are no longer relegated to the background but are placed at the very heart of the narrative.

Around the same time social historians began broadening their research to include women and other previously neglected elements of society, the feminist movement of the late 1960s and 1970s was also bringing unprecedented attention to the female heritage. Feminists hoped that by examining women's past experiences, contemporary women could better understand why and how gender-based expectations had developed in their societies, as well as how they might reshape inherited—and typically restrictive—economic, social, and political roles in the future.

Today, some four decades after the feminist and social history movements gave new impetus to the study of women's history, there is a rich and continually growing body of work on all aspects of women's lives in the past. The Lucent Books Women in History series draws upon this abundant and diverse literature to introduce students to women's experiences within a variety of past cultures and time periods in terms of the distinct roles they filled. In their capacities as workers, activists, and artists, women exerted significant influence on important events whether they conformed to or broke from traditional roles. The Women in History titles depict extraordinary women who managed to attain positions of influence in their male-dominated societies, including such celebrated heroines as the feisty medieval queen Eleanor of Aquitaine, the brilliant propagandist of the American Revolution Mercy Otis Warren, and the courageous African American activist of the Civil War era Harriet Tubman. Included as well are the stories of the ordinary—and often overlooked—women of the past who also helped shape their societies myriad ways—moral, intellectual, and economic—without straying far from customary gender roles: the housewives and mothers, school teachers and church volunteers, midwives and nurses and wartime camp followers.

In this series, readers will discover that many of these unsung women took more significant parts in the great political and social upheavals of their day than has often been recognized. In *Women of the American Revolution,* for example, students will learn how American housewives assumed a crucial role in helping the Patriots win the war against Britain. They accomplished this by planting and harvesting fields, producing and trading goods, and doing whatever else was necessary to maintain the family farm or business in the absence of their soldier husbands despite the heavy burden of housekeeping and child-care duties they already bore. By their self-sacrificing actions, competence, and ingenuity, these anonymous heroines not only kept their families alive, but kept the economy of their struggling young nation going as well during eight long years of war.

Each volume in this series contains generous commentary from the works of respected contemporary scholars, but the Women in History series particularly emphasizes quotations from primary sources such as diaries, letters, and journals whenever possible to allow the women of the past to speak for themselves. These firsthand accounts not only help students to better understand the dimensions of women's daily spheres—the work they did, the organizations they belonged to, the physical hardships they faced—but also how they viewed themselves and their actions in the light of their society's expectations for their sex.

The distinguished American historian Mary Beard once wrote that women have always been a "force in history." It is hoped that the books in this series will help students to better appreciate the vital yet often little-known ways in which women of the past have shaped their societies and cultures.

Introduction:
The Long Struggle for Suffrage

❧

From the early decades of American colonial history, many women worked outside the home: Single women and widows ran businesses of all sorts; married women took care of their husbands' estates while they were away on business, at war, or tending to affairs of state. With greater independence came the increasing conviction among such women that in a democratic society women should have the right to vote. Margaret Brent, a wealthy businesswoman who owned an estate in Maryland, claimed this right as early as 1648, as did a handful of women in New Jersey and elsewhere in the decades to come.

But the few women who ventured to the polls during America's first century were glaring exceptions. Most women—and men—accepted without question the assumption that a woman's role was to take care of her home and family, not to participate in politics in any way. In an era when it was considered scandalous for a woman to speak in public, to travel unattended, or to mingle with male society,

giving women the vote was considered ludicrous. Women were thought to be incapable of understanding politics, mathematics, science, or other higher subjects. "Why exclude women [from the vote]?" asked statesman John Adams rhetorically in a letter to a colleague. "Because their delicacy renders them unfit for practice and experience in the great businesses of life, and the hardy enterprises of war. . . . Besides, their attention is so much engaged with the necessary nurture of their children, that nature has made them fittest for domestic cares."[1]

From Margaret Brent's first attempt to vote in 1648, two hundred years would pass before anyone earnestly considered the question of woman suffrage as an option. Even then, at an 1848 meeting in Seneca Falls, New York, which has become known as the birthplace of the woman suffrage movement, only some of those who had come to discuss women's rights agreed that woman suffrage was viable, or even desirable. Another seven decades would pass before women would convince others to guarantee women the right to suffrage in the form of a constitutional amendment.

The first generation of woman suffragists died without seeing their dreams fulfilled. Only one woman who was present at the famous Seneca Falls Convention in 1848 lived long enough to be able to cast her vote. But they passed on a legacy of commitment to woman suffrage that those who followed them respected and emulated.

Against High Odds

Of course, not all men were opposed to giving women the vote. From the beginning there were men who played critical

Elizabeth Cady Stanton addresses the crowd at the Seneca Falls Convention in 1848. Stanton was among the first champions of woman suffrage.

roles in the woman suffrage movement. The famous abolitionists Frederick Douglass and Henry Blackwell, who married suffragist Lucy Stone, were among those who worked intently on behalf of women. When the Anthony amendment was finally passed by Congress in 1919, several congressmen left their sickbeds—and one his wife's deathbed—to make sure they voted for the measure. However, it was women who kept the movement alive, who through fearless determination and steadfast commitment persuaded enough men to cast their votes on behalf of woman suffrage.

The story of the women of the American suffrage movement is one of principled activism and steadfast commitment to an ideal. Countless women of all races, religions, and socioeconomic classes struggled in countless ways to achieve one goal—to be able to cast a vote for the candidates of their choice. Carrie Chapman Catt and Nettie Rogers Shuler—two of the suffrage leaders who were there to see victory—write:

> Hundreds of women gave the accumulated possibilities of an entire lifetime, thousands gave years of their lives, hundreds of thousands gave constant interest and such aid as they could. It was a continuous, seemingly endless, chain of activity. Young suffragists who helped forge the last links

"Remember the Ladies!"

Abigail Adams is often considered among the earliest American feminists. In a 1776 letter to her husband John, who was at the Continental Congress deciding the direction of the American colonies, she asked him to "Remember the Ladies" in crafting a new government. Some historians refer to John Adams's response as good-natured bantering; others interpret it as derisive ridicule. Regardless, it is clear that he did not take seriously her request for equal rights under the law. The following excerpts are from "Ourselves and Our Daughters Forever," an essay by Linda K. Kerber appearing in Marjorie Spruill Wheeler's *One Woman, One Vote*. (The original spelling and usage has been kept intact.)

Abigail Adams to John Adams,
March 31, 1776:

In the new Code of Laws which I suppose it will be necessary for you to make, I desire you would Remember the Ladies, and be more generous and favourable to them than your ancestors. Do not put such unlimited power into the hands of the Husbands. Remember all Men would be tyrants if they could. If perticular care and attention is not paid to the Ladies, we are determined to foment a Rebelion, and will not hold ourselves bound by any Laws in which we have no voice, or Representation.

That your Sex are Naturally Tyrannical is a Truth so thoroughly established as to admit of no dispute. . . . Why, then, not put it out of the power of the vicious and the Lawless to use us with cruelty and indignity with impunity?

John Adams to Abigail Adams,
April 14, 1776:

As to your extraordinary Code of Laws, I cannot but laugh. We have been told that our struggle has loosened the bonds of Government every where. That Children and Apprentices were disobedient—that schools and colleges were grown turbulent—that Indians slighted their guardians and Negroes grew insolent to their Masters. But your Letter was the first Intimation that another Tribe more numerous and powerfull than all the rest were grown discontented. . . . Depend upon it, We know better than to repeal our Masculine systems. . . . We have only the Name of Masters, and rather than give up this, which would completely subject Us to the Despotism of the Peticoat, I hope General Washington, and all our brave Heroes would fight.

Women stand in line with men in New York in 1920 to cast their vote. The election of 1920 was the first in which the federal government allowed women in all states to vote.

of that chain were not born when it began. Old suffragists who forged the first links were dead when it ended. [2]

The suffragists fought for the vote with any weapons they could find. They collected signatures on petitions to local, state, and national legislatures. They testified at legislative hearings. They toured endlessly, giving lectures on woman suffrage as a right and as a tool for improving governance. They wrote articles for whatever publications would print them and began their own publications when these were too few.

Over time, suffragist tactics grew more confrontational. Militant suffragists looked for opportunities to attract attention to their cause. They organized parades, rallies, and open-air meetings. They picketed Congress and the White House. When they were sentenced to jail, they even went on hunger strikes to protest their treatment.

Sweet Success

By the early 1900s, politicians who tried to ignore the women who claimed the right to vote often found themselves on the wrong side of public opinion. The United States of America was far different from the pre–Civil War republic in which slavery was an established institution and women's roles were significantly restricted. Women had moved from their homes into the work world, both in factories and in professions. Women in increasing numbers were voting in the states that had granted them the right. Women were doctors, lawyers, writers, social workers. Once Jeannette Rankin of Montana was elected to the House of Representatives, there was even a woman in Congress.

And, in 1920, women finally won the constitutional protection they had sought for seventy years.

Chapter 1:
Pioneers for
Woman Suffrage

The first suffragists played a critical role in inspiring women to talk—or even think—about participating in American democratic politics and seeking equal civil rights. They fought against seemingly intractable beliefs and societal conventions of the mid-1800s. Early suffragists rose from the ranks of reformers advocating great changes in society, particularly the abolition of slavery; in the process their struggles became inextricably linked. As female reformers fought to speak out on the issues that so consumed their attention, they fought for their right to speak as women. The experience taught them there was little they could do without political power—power wielded by the vote. These women planted the seeds of a slow revolution of thought and action, gradually moving the issue of woman suffrage from the sidelines to center stage.

Most early–nineteenth-century American women focused on caring for their families and households and left politics to men. Women's social life centered on church-related and family gatherings. By midcentury, lectures, debates, and meetings on various causes ranked among the most common social events for women. Women who had been inspired to activism in the causes of the prohibition of alcohol, helping the poor, and especially the abolition of slavery became the pioneers of the cause of woman suffrage.

Roots in the Antislavery Movement

Moved by personal conviction and the urge to remedy what they saw as social ills, women began to speak their minds outside the home, but they were silenced by the laws that prohibited them from political participation. They soon found themselves moving beyond fighting for the issues they cared about so deeply to fighting for their own right to speak on such issues. Sarah and Angelina Grimké, sisters from South Carolina who had moved north to fight for abolition, were perhaps among the first women to fight for their right to speak out. When the Grimkés participated in an antislavery campaign in

Massachusetts in the summer of 1837, Congregationalist ministers attacked their behavior as unladylike and unchristian. "When [a woman] assumes the place and tone of man as a public reformer," the ministers wrote in a circular, "she yields the power which God has given her for her protection, and her character becomes unnatural."[3]

Angelina Grimké recognized that women would be able to do little to improve the rights of others without obtaining rights of their own. In response to suggestions that they should refrain from making public appearances, she wrote, "If we surrender the right to speak in public this year, we must surrender the right to petition next year, and the right to write the year after, and so on. What then can woman do for the slave, when she herself is under the feet of man and shamed into silence?"[4] Thus, as the Grimkés struggled to defend their right to speak on behalf of enslaved blacks, they found themselves defending their right to speak on behalf of their own rights. "We are placed very unexpectedly in a very trying situation, in the forefront of an entirely new contest," wrote Angelina, "a contest for the rights of woman as a moral, intelligent and responsible being."[5]

The Grimkés were not the only advocates for women's rights who were culled from the ranks of activists. Women abolitionists were often active participants in the male-dominated antislavery societies that were cropping up throughout the northern United States, but at meetings they were usually prohibited from voting and sometimes even speaking. They soon found themselves drawn together in the struggle for their own rights.

Angelina Grimké was an abolitionist before becoming an advocate for women's rights.

The antislavery movement not only showed women that they lacked rights and political power but taught them many of the skills they needed to obtain these rights. In 1833, when women were denied membership in the newly formed American Anti-Slavery Society, a group of female abolitionists in Philadelphia formed their own abolitionist group. In her book on the women of the Seneca Falls Convention, Miriam Gurko discusses the impact of the female antislavery societies, "The ladies who were later to work for woman's rights . . . learned how to organize and work together, and how to handle the vociferous criticism they received. They learned the techniques of circulating petitions and holding conventions. They learned how to take direct and often dangerous action. . . . Above all, they learned to speak before an audience."[6]

An Idea Takes Hold

Among the more prominent female abolitionists was Lucretia Coffin Mott. Mott was a traditional wife (of a leading abolitionist) and mother, but her work in the antislavery movement would lead to a growing passion for women's rights until, she says, it became "the most important question in my life."[7]

Lucretia Mott's commitment to women's rights was fueled in part by her friendship with Elizabeth Cady Stanton—a friendship born at the World Anti-Slavery Convention held in 1840 in London, England. Stanton was in attendance with her new husband, who was a delegate to the convention. Mott was one of several female members of the American delegation. Although these women were selected because of their leadership in the antislavery movement, they soon learned that, once again, they would be prohibited from participation simply because of their sex. When the convention opened, some of the male delegates contended that the

Lucretia Coffin Mott was a prominent abolitionist who became involved with women's rights after she befriended Elizabeth Cady Stanton.

women should not be allowed to participate. After a brief debate (from which the
women were excluded), they were denied
a voice and directed to seats in the gallery.

Denied a role in the meeting, Stanton
and Mott took to taking long walks
through the city. Although Mott was over
twenty years older than Stanton, the two
learned they had much in common,
including not only their abhorrence of
slavery but their frustration that they were
unable to change things simply because
they were women. When they parted ways
at the end of the convention, they agreed
to meet again to further discuss what they
could do to advance their cause. Although
it would be eight years before they would
meet again, both Stanton and Mott continued to think about how they could best
improve the plight of women.

The Seeds of Discontent

As she settled into family life, Elizabeth
Cady Stanton grew increasingly unsatisfied
with the drudgery of housework and raising a growing family. Her husband traveled
often, and there were few distractions in the
small Upstate New York town in which
they lived. Elizabeth, like so many of her
contemporaries, felt unfulfilled by the constant demands of caring for a family and
running a household. She later wrote:

I now fully understood the practical
difficulties most women had to con-
tend with in the isolated household.
. . . The general discontent I felt with
woman's portion as wife, mother,
housekeeper, physician, and spiritual
guide, and the chaotic conditions
into which everything fell without
her constant supervision, and the
wearied, anxious look of the majority of women impressed me with a
strong feeling that some active measures should be taken. . . . I could not
see what to do or where to begin—
my only thought was a public meeting for protest and discussion.[8]

In 1848 Elizabeth Cady Stanton received word that Lucretia Mott was planning to visit her sister in a nearby town.
Although she had not seen Mott for eight
years, the two women had continued to
exchange letters, and Stanton was eager for
the opportunity to meet again. As Stanton
visited with Lucretia Mott, Martha C.
Wright (Mott's sister), and Mary Ann
McClintock, she began to talk about how
unhappy she was. "I poured out, that day,
the torrent of my accumulating discontent,
with such vehemence and indignation that
I stirred myself, as well as the rest of the
party, to do and dare anything,"[9] she wrote
later.

Stanton's audience was sympathetic.
They each had experienced similar frustrations in their lives as wives, mothers,
caretakers—that is, in their lives as women.
And they had talked to many other

Elizabeth Cady Stanton

Elizabeth Cady Stanton is often considered the founder of the woman suffrage movement. The daughter of a prominent lawyer in Upstate New York, she often visited her father's law office, and she became convinced that changing the laws was the only way to improve life for women. At age twenty-five, she married abolitionist leader Henry Stanton and accompanied him to the 1840 World Anti-Slavery Convention in London. There, she met Lucretia Mott, a woman twenty years her senior who shared her passion for women's rights. After an eight-year correspondence, the two met for coffee in Upstate New York and agreed to hold a meeting on the topic. The result, the Seneca Falls Convention of 1848, immediately brought Stanton national attention.

Stanton met Susan B. Anthony in 1851. The two women worked together to build and lead the woman suffrage movement for decades. A skilled writer, Stanton often served as the voice behind Anthony as well as other woman suffrage orators. Her ideas sometimes proved to be too radical for her contemporaries. She shocked many of those around her with her resolution to secure the vote at the Seneca Falls Convention. Her *Woman's Bible,* a critique of Christianity's view of women published in 1895, was similarly met with reproach. Stanton also was instrumental in preserving much of the history of the movement in books and journals, including *The History of the Woman Suffrage Movement* and *Eighty Years and More.*

women who felt the same way. Perhaps, Elizabeth posed, something could be done to remedy that frustration.

A "Ridiculous" Notion

The women agreed that a first step would be to talk to other women about the plight and the rights of women. Recognizing that they needed a forum to air their issues, they decided to hold a meeting open to all. Stanton placed an advertisement in the local *Seneca Falls Courier:*

WOMAN'S RIGHTS CONVENTION—A Convention to discuss the social, civil, and religious condition and rights of women, will be held in the Wesleyan Chapel, at Seneca Falls, N. Y., on Wednesday and Thursday, the 19th and 20th of July, current; commencing at 10 o'clock A.M. During the first day the meeting will be exclusively for women, who are earnestly invited to attend. The public generally are invited to be present on the second day, when Lucretia Mott, of Philadelphia, and other ladies and gentlemen, will address the convention. [10]

At first the women planning the convention were at a loss to organize such a meeting. But as Stanton read aloud the Declaration of Independence, they had an idea. They could follow the format of that most important American historical document to argue that democratic principles necessarily applied to women. Stanton went through the Declaration of Independence and inserted the word *women* where appropriate. "We hold these truths to be self-evident that all men *and women* are created equal," [11] the new document declared. The women then listed grievances, again modeling their document after the Declaration of Independence.

Stanton was then asked to list resolutions that would establish women as equals with men. Her twelve resolutions included demands for the rights to gain an education, to own property, to control one's own earnings, to share in the custody of children after divorce, and to be heard in court. There was one more demand: the right to vote. Giving women the right to vote was a shocking idea. Her husband, Henry Stanton, vowed to leave town if she presented this as part of the resolutions at the convention (a threat he carried out). Even Lucretia Mott feared that asking for the vote went too far. "Thou will make

us ridiculous," she warned. "We must go slowly." [12]

The Seneca Falls Convention

There was little advance publicity for the meeting, but, much to the surprise of the organizers, more than three hundred people—including about forty men— came from as far as fifty miles away. The attendees were from different communities and different walks of life. Most were middle-class and married, but among their ranks were also working women and domestics who shared a sense of dissatisfaction with the unequal status of women.

Charlotte Woodward, a nineteen-year-old school teacher who did piece-work for a glove factory in Waterloo, New York, explained her reason for attendance: "Every fibre of my being rebelled, although silently, all the hours that I sat and sewed gloves for a miserable pittance which, after it was earned, could never be mine. I wanted to work, but I wanted to choose my task and I wanted to collect my wages." [13]

On the first day, when attendance was limited to women only, the participants debated the rights that women should have and the obstacles women faced in securing such rights and listened to speeches about what forms protest should or should not take. The second day's proceeding's, led by men, featured Elizabeth

Cady Stanton's reading of the Declaration of Sentiments. The document was met with enthusiasm. Put to a vote, eleven of the resolutions were passed unanimously. The only clause that was contested was Resolution 9: "Resolved, that it is the duty of the women of this country to secure to themselves their sacred right to the elective franchise [the right to vote]."[14] Many people in the audience were shocked by this proposal to give women the vote, but after much debate and the passionate endorsement of Stanton and Frederick Douglass, the famous abolitionist, the resolution was adopted by a narrow margin.

One hundred people—sixty-eight women and thirty-two men—affixed their names to the Declaration of Sentiments. Charlotte Woodward would be the only one present who would live long enough to see their wish for woman suffrage fulfilled.

The Aftermath

The meeting at Seneca Falls brought a storm of protest. Newspapers attacked and ridiculed the women for their bold declarations. "There is no danger of the Woman Question dying for want of notice," wrote Elizabeth Cady Stanton in

The Wesleyan Chapel in Seneca Falls, New York (pictured), was the site of the first Women's Rights Convention in 1848.

Women of the Suffrage Movement

Seneca Falls Resolutions

❦

One hundred women and men who came to Seneca Falls signed a series of resolutions modeled after the Declaration of Independence. The following excerpt listing some of these resolutions is from an account of the Seneca Falls Convention written in 1881 by Elizabeth Cady Stanton, Susan B. Anthony, and Matilda Joslyn Gage in the first volume of *The History of the Woman Suffrage Movement*.

Resolved, That all laws which prevent woman from occupying such a station in society as her conscience shall dictate, or which place her in a position inferior to that of man, are contrary to the great precept of nature, and therefore of no force or authority.

Resolved, That woman is man's equal—was intended to be so by the Creator, and the highest good of the race demands that she should be recognized as such. . . .

Resolved, That inasmuch as man, while claiming for himself intellectual superiority, does accord to woman moral superiority, it is preeminently his duty to encourage her to speak and teach, as she has an opportunity, in all religious assemblies. . . .

Resolved, That woman has too long rested satisfied in the circumscribed limits which corrupt customs and a perverted application of the Scriptures have marked out for her, and that it is time she should move in the enlarged sphere which her great Creator has assigned her.

Resolved, that it is the duty of the women of this country to secure to themselves their sacred right to the elective franchise. . . .

Resolved, That the speedy success of our cause depends upon the zealous and untiring efforts of both men and women, for the overthrow of the monopoly of the pulpit, and for the securing to woman an equal participation with men in the various trades, professions and commerce.

The only resolution that was not unanimously adopted was the ninth, urging the women of the country to secure to themselves the elective franchise. Those who took part in the debate feared a demand for the right to vote would defeat others they deemed more rational, and make the whole movement ridiculous.

But Mrs. Stanton and Frederick Douglass, seeing that the power to choose rulers and make laws was the right by which all others could be secured, persistently advocated the resolution, and at last carried it by a small majority.

a letter. "Every paper you take up has something to say about it."[15] The women who attended the convention were accused of undermining the family and ignoring their responsibilities. One editorial called the convention "the most shocking and unnatural incident ever recorded in the history of womanity."[16]

Expanding Women's Rights

Suffrage was not the only right that women were denied in nineteenth-century America. Before the 1830s, women in most places could not own property or sign legal contracts, could not sue in a court of law or win custody of their children during a divorce. Beginning in the 1830s, however, states began to heed the demands of pioneering women activists and concede the right of women to own property. The following excerpt from the New York State Married Women's Property Act, reprinted from Linda K. Kerber, "Ourselves and Our Daughters Forever," an essay in Marjorie Spruill Wheeler's *One Woman, One Vote,* is typical of this type of legislation. Laws such as this set important precedents for the suffrage legislation to come.

The real and personal property of any female [now married and] who may hereafter marry, and which she shall own at the time of marriage, and the rents, issues and profits thereof shall not be subject to the disposal of her husband, nor be liable for his debts, and shall continue her sole and separate property, as if she were a single female. . . . It shall be lawful for any married female to receive by gift, grant, devise or bequest, from any person other than her husband and hold to her sole and separate use, as if she were a single female, real and personal property, and the rents, issues and profits thereof and the same shall not be subject to the disposal of her husband, nor be liable for his debts. . . .

A married woman may bargain, sell, assign, and transfer her separate personal property, and carry on any trade or business, and perform any labor or services on her sole and separate account, and the earnings of any married woman from her trade . . . shall be her sole and separate property, and may be used or invested by her in her own name.

Any married woman may, while married, sue and be sued in all matters having relations to her . . . sole and separate property. . . .

Every married woman is hereby constituted and declared to be the joint guardian of her children, with her husband, with equal powers, rights, and duties in regard to them, with the husband.

Women of the Suffrage Movement

In the face of such outrage, some women backed down from the cause. Some even asked to have their signatures removed from the declaration. But most stood firm. In fact, the criticism served to strengthen their resolve.

The ideas put forth at Seneca Falls struck a chord in many women. Emily Collins, who lived in nearby South Bristol, New York, wrote:

> From the earliest dawn of reason I pined for that freedom of thought and action that was then denied to all womankind. I revolted in spirit against the customs of society and the laws of the State that crushed my aspirations and debarred me from the pursuit of almost every object worthy of an intelligent, rational mind. But not until that meeting at Seneca Falls in 1848 ...gave this feeling of unrest form and voice, did I take action.[17]

Collins would respond to the call for action by organizing fifteen of her neighbors into an equal rights society and petitioning the legislature for the vote.

A "Golden Age"

Just two weeks after the Seneca Falls Convention, some of the women participants helped organize another women's rights convention in nearby Rochester, New York. Rather than having men lead the proceedings, as at Seneca Falls, the organizers appointed a woman to preside over the meeting. Support for this step was weak: Mott, Stanton, and McClintock were among those who considered having a woman president a "most hazardous experiment." Stanton later recollected their concerns: "To write a Declaration and Resolutions, to make a speech, and debate had taxed their powers to the uttermost; and now, with such feeble voices and timid manners, without the slightest knowledge of [procedural rules], or the least experience in public meetings, how could a woman preside?"[18]

Before long, however, similar meetings were held in Ohio, Massachusetts, Indiana, Pennsylvania, and at other places in New York. The first National Women's Rights Convention, held in Worcester, Massachusetts, in 1850, attracted more than a thousand people from as far away as California. For the next ten years, national women's conventions were held every year except 1857. Hardly two months went by without a state convention somewhere, and hundreds of smaller gatherings were held in small towns and big cities throughout the country. One women's history expert dubs the decade "a 'golden age' of woman suffrage activity."[19]

Many of the women who attended these early meetings came from miles away, traveling for hours by carriage or on foot—walking six, eight, and ten miles simply for the opportunity to talk to others about what could be done to advance the cause of women. Some of the meetings attracted so much attention that people had to be turned away at the door for lack of room.

As women began openly to talk about suffrage, the idea began to seem less ridiculous—and more necessary. While the women's movement at first tended to focus on issues that directly affected women's quality of life, such as property rights and education, an increasing number of advocates saw the right to vote as the best way to safeguard advances in these areas. A resolution taken at the 1856 national convention read: "Resolved, that the main power of the woman's rights movement lies in this: that while always demanding for woman better education, better employment, and better laws, it has kept steadily in view the one cardinal demand for the right of suffrage: in a democracy, the symbol and guarantee of all other rights."[20]

No longer were such resolutions met by a hushed silence or vigorous debate; rather, suffrage became a critical right that women's rights advocates added to their list of demands. "After the Seneca Falls Convention, there is no further evidence of reluctance within the movement to demand the vote," writes Ellen Carol DuBois. "On the contrary, it quickly became the cornerstone of the women's rights program."[21]

Taking Action

Although the spate of such meetings led some contemporaries to claim that all the

Elizabeth Cady Stanton poses with her daughter Harriot. Stanton firmly believed that the right of suffrage should be the most important demand of the women's rights movement.

women did was talk, the women at the conventions began to forge plans for collective action. In 1854 in New York, for example, women organized a midwinter campaign to petition the legislature for rights, including the vote. In just ten weeks, the women collected over six thousand signatures.

The challenges to gaining signatures were formidable. Travel accommodations were primitive. Due to society's conventions against a woman traveling alone, it was often difficult for the women canvassers to find a decent meal and acceptable accommodations. They were often met with hostility or disdain by the people who answered the door. A biographer of Susan B. Anthony describes the situation:

Like itinerant tin pedlars or book agents they tramped the streets and country roads, knocking at every door, presenting their petitions, arguing with women who half the time slammed the door in their faces with the smug remark that they had husbands, thank God, to look after their interests, and they needed no new laws to protect their rights. After each rebuff the women simply trudged on to the next street, the next row of houses, the next grudgingly opened front door. [22]

The Legacy

It is perhaps hard to appreciate today the courage it took to organize and speak at these women's rights meetings. Even in attending such meetings, women faced vociferous opposition of community and church leaders, as well as friends and family—often women as well as men. The pioneer suffragists dared to stand up for themselves in an era in which this was considered unladylike and improper. Author Ellen Carol DuBois writes:

> While many accounts of this first generation of feminist activists stress what distinguishes them from other women—their bravery and open rebellion—it is equally important to recognize what they had in common with [all women of the time]: lack of public skills; lives marked by excessive domesticity; husbands and fathers hostile to their efforts; the material pressures of housekeeping and child-rearing; and the deep psychological insecurity bred by all these factors. [23]

Elizabeth Cady Stanton's husband criticized her suffrage work, and her father carried out a threat to disown her after she spoke at a woman suffrage rally (a move he later reversed by putting her back into his will).

Slowly, women began to make strides toward earning equal rights. The New York legislature passed a women's rights bill in 1860, and other states soon followed. The women engaged in the early days of the fight broke down barriers to women voicing their political opinions, speaking in public, and traveling alone. Perhaps most important was the contribution of the first suffragists as role models. Many of the women who devoted their lives to gaining the vote were inspired by hearing a woman speak before an audience.

The first women's rights advocates drew strength from one another. Barred from participation in political life, many educated women formed informal debating and speaking societies, where they practiced framing arguments and speaking before a group. As a next step, they would organize into national, regional, state, and local groups that had but one goal—a goal shared by those who had come before them: to secure power through the vote.

Chapter 2:
National Organizers and the Political Struggle

❧

Born of the antislavery movement, woman suffrage quickly moved beyond its abolitionist roots, and the women who had played a critical role in gaining freedom for slaves began to organize on behalf of woman suffrage. In an essay on the period following the Civil War, Andrea Moore Kerr writes, "Loosely organized under the leadership of Lucy Stone, Elizabeth Cady Stanton, and Susan B. Anthony, women raised funds and managed finances, organized conventions, developed strategies, delineated goals, and determined the direction of the movement."[24] Anthony, Stanton, and Stone quickly became nationally recognized leaders of the woman suffrage movement. They were the thinkers behind the movement—the women who vehemently defended a woman's right to vote and outlined the arguments that would be used to convince others. They also determined the strategies that would be used to secure woman suffrage.

The informal, ad hoc groups that struggled to define the woman suffrage agenda following the Civil War soon grew into strong national membership organizations. The women of the National Woman Suffrage Association (NWSA) and American Woman Suffrage Association (AWSA) became instrumental in providing a means for sharing ideas, carving out strategies, and providing leadership. With funds from women's rights meetings and speaking engagements, the NWSA and AWSA published and distributed books, pamphlets, and posters defining the reasons that men should give women the right to vote. They made woman suffrage a national issue, lobbying the U.S. Congress and demanding a constitutional amendment that would protect a woman's right to vote. The two organizations settled their differences and merged in 1890 to become the National American Woman Suffrage Association (NAWSA). With Susan B. Anthony as its first president and Elizabeth Cady Stanton as vice president, the NAWSA continued lobbying efforts on both the national and state levels.

The women who led these national organizations became the country's first "professional" suffragists. They tended to be well-educated people skilled in many leadership roles, especially speaking, writing, planning, and organizing. Most were paid representatives of suffrage organizations and received compensation for their speaking engagements, but money was not the driving force behind their commitment. Woman suffrage organizations typically operated on shoestring budgets and had but few funds to pay their leaders. Those who could afford to do so often denied payment and donated the earnings from their speaking engagements to the movement. Early in her affiliation with the movement, Susan B. Anthony worked for just twelve dollars a week, saving on expenses by staying with acquaintances when traveling, spending just a few cents on meals, and traveling on foot from one end of the city to another.

Susan B. Anthony Joins the Movement

One of the largest and most effective national organizations was the NWSA, established in 1869 by Susan B. Anthony and Elizabeth Cady Stanton. Anthony and Stanton shared a passion for woman suffrage and women's rights. Anthony held a deep conviction that women should have the same rights as men. When she was a teacher, she spoke out against the injustice of a system in which women were paid less than their male counterparts and against the rules that denied female teachers a voice at meetings. As an agent for the abolitionist movement, Anthony also helped to break down many perceptions of what was considered appropriate behavior for women. Her work in the abolitionist movement necessitated that she travel extensively, and she often dined solo or spent the night by herself in a hotel.

Susan B. Anthony (left) and Elizabeth Cady Stanton created the National Woman Suffrage Association to make suffrage a constitutional amendment.

Susan B. Anthony

Susan B. Anthony, the best-known and most-loved suffragist, was born to a Quaker family in western Massachusetts and spent most of her life in Upstate New York. Anthony taught school as a young woman but quit in protest over the practice of paying women teachers far less than their male colleagues. She was alarmed about the fate of women under a legal system that failed to protect them against alcoholic husbands who squandered their money on drink, gambling, and other women. She joined the temperance movement in 1848, where she became a voice for changes in the law that would put more power in the hands of women. In 1856 Anthony's reform efforts had shifted to the abolition of slavery, and she took a job with the American Anti-Slavery Society, organizing meetings and giving lectures.

An ardent reformer, Anthony never lost sight of the importance of empowering women. In part due to her work, the New York state legislature passed a women's rights bill in 1860, giving women the right to own property, to file lawsuits, and to share in the custody of children after a divorce. After teaming up with Elizabeth Cady Stanton and other suffragists in 1851, Anthony gave decades of single-minded dedication to the cause of suffrage, proving to be an adept organizer and persuasive communicator. She worked tirelessly for women's rights and woman suffrage in her home state of New York and on a national level.

Anthony believed that the best way to secure the vote was through a constitutional amendment and worked wholeheartedly toward this goal—first, by attempting to name sex as one of the protected categories covered by the Fifteenth Amendment and, later, by encouraging the adoption of a separate amendment. When the so-called Anthony amendment was finally introduced to Congress in 1878, Anthony led deputations to Washington year after year to lobby on its behalf.

In 1872 she twice led women to the polls to vote, and she was subsequently arrested and fined for violating voting laws. She founded and led the National Woman Suffrage Association before it merged with the American Woman Suffrage Association in 1890 and then served as the first president of the newly merged National American Woman Suffrage Association. Although women were not granted the right to vote until almost fifteen years after Anthony's death in 1906, Susan B. Anthony played a critical role in achieving enfranchisement.

Many people who had believed that it was dangerous or scandalous for women to travel alone began to change their opinions.

Stanton and Anthony accomplished far more together than either of them would have alone. Anthony brought to the movement organizing skills and experience; Stanton provided the philosophical framework and carved out the arguments they would use. Stanton later wrote: "In writing we did better work together than either could alone. While she is slow and analytical in composition, I am rapid and synthetic. I am the better writer, she the better critic. She supplied the facts and statistics, I the philosophy and rhetoric, and together we have made arguments that have stood unshaken by the storms of thirty long years."[25]

As the country debated the issue of granting suffrage to newly freed slaves after the Civil War, the NWSA argued that women should be given the same rights as African Americans. The petition to the U.S. Congress to have women included in the Fifteenth Amendment marked the first time a petition was submitted to Congress rather than to state legislatures. It read in part: "As you are now amending the Constitution, and, in harmony with advancing civilization, placing new safeguards round the individual rights of four million of emancipated ex-slaves, we ask that you extend the right of Suffrage to Woman . . . and thus fulfill your constitutional obligation to guarantee to every State in the Union a Republican form of Government."[26] When the crafters of the amendment refused to include sex among the factors that could not be used to determine who could vote, the NWSA set out to oppose its passage.

Suffrage for All, but for Ex-Slaves First

Some suffragists did not agree that they should oppose a constitutional amendment giving suffrage for black men. Securing the vote for black males would pave the way for women, they argued. Lucy Stone, an abolitionist and women's rights activist, and Julia Ward Howe, a leader of the women's club movement who gained national acclaim as the author of the "Battle Hymn of the Republic," were among those who made this argument. "I think it is a great pity to try and create or give currency to the idea that the Woman's Movement is opposed to the Fifteenth Amendment," wrote Stone. "It is not true that our movement is opposed to the negro. But it will be very easy to make it so, to the mutual harm of both causes."[27]

Lucy Stone and Julia Ward Howe wanted to continue to push for woman suffrage but opposed what they viewed as the radical tactics of the newly formed NWSA. At the next meeting of the New England Woman Suffrage Association, in which Stone and Howe played a leadership role, they formed their own rival organization. The AWSA declared as its purpose securing the ballot for women, based upon the belief that "suffrage for woman is the great key that will unlock to her the doors of social and political equality." The AWSA proposed to organize for suffrage state by state and to "prepare and circulate petitions to State Legislatures, to Congress, or to constitutional conventions in behalf of the legal and political equality of women."[28] At the 1870 AWSA meeting, resolutions were passed to continue the state organizational work while supporting the adoption of a federal constitutional amendment.

Lobbying for Change

The leaders of the NWSA scorned this state-by-state approach. Anthony and Stanton instead intensified their efforts to secure the passage of a constitutional amendment.

Much has been made about the ideological differences between these two organizations. Under the leadership of Anthony and Stanton, the NWSA demanded sweeping social change to improve the status of women—a revolution in thought and action. The AWSA, under the leadership of Stone and Howe, favored a more moderate approach. "Their periodical, *The Woman's Journal,* had a polite, literary tone and did not stray far

from 'woman's sphere,'" writes historian Edith Mayo, "although they did call for voting rights."[29]

Despite their philosophical differences, however, the two major national woman suffrage organizations had much in common. First and foremost, the national leaders focused on convincing others that women should have the right to vote and on bringing others into the movement. In addition to their own newspapers, the women of the national organizations defined their arguments in myriad newspaper editorials and magazine articles, as well as posters, pamphlets, and advertisements. To support these efforts, the national organizers had to continually engage in fund-raising campaigns and look for wealthy benefactors. In the 1880s, for example, the AWSA staged a series of "bazaars" in Boston. Hundreds of volunteers donated their time, skills, and goods to raise money for woman suffrage. Crowds drawn by the plays, music, and art gallery could peruse the donated merchandise, consisting of everything from handmade crafts to pianos and from dried fish and soap to washing machines and cooking stoves.

The Anthony Amendment

The NWSA continued to push for a constitutional amendment that would grant women suffrage nationwide. In 1877 Susan B. Anthony delivered to the U.S.

Lucy Stone

Lucy Stone, an ardent abolitionist and feminist, is perhaps remembered most for being the first woman in the United States to keep her own name after marriage. In the 1855 marriage ceremony, bride Lucy Stone and groom Henry Blackwell issued a statement renouncing and protesting the marriage laws of the time. Blackwell joined Stone in her fight for women's rights, traveling throughout the country on behalf of the cause.

Stone was born into a family of Massachusetts farmers in 1818. An avid student, Lucy learned faster than her brother, who went on to college, but her father would not support her education, so she became a teacher and did housework to earn enough money for college. She attended Mount Holyoke Female Seminary in 1839, and in 1843 she enrolled in Oberlin College in Ohio, the country's first college to admit both women and blacks. She graduated in 1847, becoming the first woman in Massachusetts to earn a college degree.

After becoming an agent for the American Anti-Slavery Society, she included in her speeches a plea for women's rights. But this created controversy within the Anti-Slavery Society because some people felt it took attention away from the cause of abolition. So she arranged to speak on weekends on abolition and weekdays on women's rights. Her radicalism on both subjects brought large crowds, many of whom were opposed to her ideas. To support the latter endeavor, she charged admission for her speeches, earning seven thousand dollars in just three years.

In 1850 Stone was a leader in organizing the first National Women's Rights Convention, held in Worcester, Massachusetts. She was also among the founders of the American Woman Suffrage Association and continued to lecture and write on behalf of woman suffrage until her death in 1893.

Lucy Stone divided her time between championing abolition and advocating women's rights.

Senate ten thousand signatures demanding the right to vote—an action that was met by laughter in the Senate. The next year, Senator Aaron Sargent of California proposed a woman suffrage amendment. The proposal read simply, "The right of citizens of the United States to vote shall not be denied or abridged by the United States or any state on account of sex." [30]

For the most part, Congress reacted to the petitions for a constitutional amendment with ridicule and disdain. Elizabeth Stanton headed the women witnesses who argued for the proposal before the Senate Committee on Privileges and Elections. Stanton later wrote:

> In the whole course of our struggle for equal rights, I never felt more exasperated than on this occasion.... The peculiarly aggravating feature of the present occasion was the studied inattention and contempt of the chairman, Senator Wadleigh of New Hampshire.... He alternately looked over some manuscripts and newspapers before him, and jumped up to open or close a door or a window. He stretched, yawned, gazed at the ceiling, cut his nails, sharpened his pencil, changing his occupation and position every two minutes, effectively preventing the establishing of the faintest magnetic current between the speakers and the committee. It was

with difficulty that I restrained the impulse more than once to hurl my manuscript at his head. [31]

The amendment failed to garner much support that year, but supporters planned to introduce it every year until it became law. Year after year, deputations of women descended on Congress to testify for what became known as the Anthony amendment. The suffragists gradually gained more support, tacit at first, among members of Congress. Several times in the 1880s, the select committees appointed to review the amendment reported on it favorably, and it finally reached the floor for debate in 1886. When the Senate voted on the amendment for the first time in 1887, however, suffragists were devastated by the news: It lost by a vote of more than two to one. Although the amendment continued to be introduced each year, the senate would not vote on it again for twenty-five years.

Organizational Alignments

The NWSA and AWSA were the most prominent woman suffrage organizations in the 1870s and 1880s, but they were strengthened by other like-minded leaders. The Woman's Christian Temperance Union (WCTU), founded in 1874 to work toward outlawing the sale of alcohol, was among the more active groups that included woman suffrage on their platforms. Under the leadership of Frances Willard, a well-educated suffrage worker,

Frances Willard used the political power of the Woman's Christian Temperance Union to sway elections on suffrage issues.

the WCTU soon became the largest women's group in the nation.

From the beginning Willard recognized the power of the WCTU to galvanize the women's rights movement. According to one biographer, Willard was drawn to the temperance movement not so much because of an overriding concern for the cause, but rather from her conviction that "it could be the means of drawing large numbers of women hitherto not receptive to the issue of greater rights for women, into activity which could lead them in that direction. Like the earlier temperance leaders, she saw that political influence would

be a determining factor in achieving their goal, and she decided to combine the two." [32]

Willard expanded the WCTU's aims to include voting rights. She explained, "We want [the ballot] because the liquor traffic is entrenched in law, and law grows out of the will of majorities, and majorities of women are against the liquor traffic." [33]

The WCTU was a well-organized group with strong political might, particularly in rural regions and small towns. In some places, temperance organizations were credited with swaying the populace in state and local elections. In bringing woman suffrage to the forefront of the WCTU's activities, Willard increased the suffrage movement's arsenal of weapons.

Carrie Chapman Catt and the NAWSA

The women who led the national organizations during the last half of the nineteenth century were inexperienced in politics and political action. Historian Andrea Moore Kerr writes, "Lacking political experience, unschooled in consensus building, without the education formed in board room and back room, woman suffragists had to learn how to gain political ground the hard way—through trial and error." [34]

But learn they did. By the end of the century, women were adept organizers and politicians. Under the guidance of the national suffrage organizations, suffragists

As president of the NAWSA, Carrie Chapman Catt pressured senators, representatives, and even the president to ratify a suffrage amendment.

islators with letters. These letters varied greatly in character: Some politely requested the vote; others demanded suffrage as a woman's constitutional right. But all conveyed the same message: Women would not stop lobbying until they had achieved their goal. The suffragists were becoming harder to ignore.

In 1916 Carrie Chapman Catt, an experienced suffragist who had led several state campaigns in the West, was chosen as president of the NAWSA. She brought new life to the national organization, which had floundered under ineffectual leadership and an ambiguous agenda. Conceding that some progress had been won in some states, Catt argued that state campaigns were draining too much energy and resources. After fifty years of endless campaigning, women had gained the right to vote in only nine states. Catt was determined that securing passage of the Anthony amendment was the only way to achieve suffrage. "We do not care a ginger snap about anything but that Federal Amendment,"[35] Catt declared.

Catt enlisted her considerable skills in grassroots organizing to build a coalition out of disparate groups. She set about reorganizing the NAWSA to bring every state and territory under its umbrella—even states that had no history of woman suffrage representation—and to bring into the membership more wealthy women who could support the cause and working

kept the issue of woman suffrage before the U.S. Congress. Women from all walks of life testified at hearings of the U.S. Congress on behalf of a woman's right to vote. In 1910, after a two-year petition drive, the National American Woman Suffrage Association (which had been created in 1890 by the merger of the NWSA and AWSA) formally presented to Congress a petition with over four hundred thousand signatures for a woman suffrage amendment. Suffrage organizations also held letter-writing campaigns, flooding the offices of national leg-

women who would give it a new sense of urgency. At the 1916 NAWSA convention, Catt called her constituents to battle:

> National Boards must be selected hereafter for one chief qualification—

the ability to lead the national fight. There should be a mobilization of at last thirty-six state armies, and these armies should move under the direction of the national officers. They

---

The National American Woman Suffrage Association

❧

This excerpt, written by Carol O'Hare, editor of *Jailed for Freedom* by Doris Stevens, describes the influence of the NAWSA.

In 1890 two rival suffrage organizations, one headed by Susan B. Anthony and Elizabeth Cady Stanton and the other by Lucy Stone and Julia Ward Howe, united to form the National American Woman Suffrage Association (NAWSA). By the time Carrie Chapman Catt was made president in 1916, NAWSA had forty-four state auxiliaries with a total membership of more than two million, but it lacked direction and effective organization.

Carrie Chapman Catt went on to become the most powerful political leader of the women's rights movement. Although her real goal was the passage of a federal suffrage amendment, she believed Congress would not act until women were able to vote in national elections in enough states to make ratification a possibility. She thus devised her "Winning Plan," which promoted work in state suffrage campaigns while simultaneously lobbying for the federal amendment.

The National American Woman Suffrage Association used very different tactics from Alice Paul and the National Woman's Party. While the NWP engaged in dramatic, militant action, NAWSA chose gentle persuasion and respectable campaigning. Both methods would prove necessary in the eventual achievement of the women's suffrage amendment, its passage by Congress, and ratification by the states.

In 1920 NAWSA became the League of Women Voters and dedicated itself to local civic matters, to the education of newly enfranchised women, and to the study of national legislation and social policy.

---

should be disciplined and obedient to the national officers in all matters concerning the national campaign.... More, those who enter on this task, should go prepared to give their lives and fortunes for success, and any pusillanimous coward among us who dares to call retreat, should be court-martialled. Any other policy than this is weak, inefficient, illogical, silly, inane, and ridiculous! Any other policy would fail of success.[36]

The "Front Door Lobby"

By now, some factions of the woman suffrage movement had begun to engage in increasingly militant tactics and to hold the party in power (the Democrats) responsible for the failure of national legislation for woman suffrage. The women who led the NAWSA, however, believed that it was far better to woo the people in power than to antagonize them through confrontation. Looking ahead to ratification, the NAWSA leaders recognized that they would need Democratic support to win over the states in the South.

Thus, the NAWSA engaged in nonpartisan politics, exerting pressure on senators, members of the House of Representatives, and the president of both parties. The press dubbed their attempts as the "Front Door Lobby" because, unlike many of the lobbyists of the day, they were open and honest about what they wanted. Women from all parts of the nation came to Washington to help the NAWSA keep watch over Congress. They kept track of what was going on at the Capitol, tallying the votes and tracking the speeches of congressmen in an attempt to identify the right words or argument that would be most persuasive—that would convince the politicians that it was politically and personally expedient for them to vote for woman suffrage.

When conservative Democrat Woodrow Wilson became president in 1912, the NAWSA focused particular attention on convincing him of the arguments for woman suffrage. Convinced that "dignified lobbying was the best way to get results,"[37] NAWSA president Carrie Chapman Catt and her lieutenant, Helen Gardener, led delegations to Washington to discuss the issue of suffrage directly with the president. They thereby became among the first women to make a formal visit to the White House.

Helen Gardener succeeded in gaining the trust of President Wilson. "Her work can rarely be reported because of its confidential nature," fellow suffragist Maud Wood Park said of Gardener, "but . . . whenever a miracle has appeared to happen in our behalf, if the facts could be told they would nearly always prove that Mrs. Gardener was the worker of wonders."[38] Gardener formed a lasting friendship with the president; when he later decided to back woman suffrage, she wrote some of his statements.

Women of the Suffrage Movement

Helen Gardner (left) and Carrie Chapman Catt leave the White House after visiting President Wilson. Wilson's endorsement of their cause led to ratification of the Anthony amendment in 1919.

Congress Debates

On January 9, 1918, President Wilson finally endorsed the Anthony amendment and urged Congress to vote in favor of the measure. The next day, Representative Jeannette Rankin of Wyoming, who was the first woman to be elected to Congress, opened the House debate. When a vote was taken at the end of the day, the amendment passed by a measure of 274 to 136, precisely the two-thirds needed for passage of a constitutional amendment. The news caused so much chaos on the floor of the House that the roll call had to be repeated three times to make sure of its accuracy.

The women crowding the galleries held their breath as the roll calls were taken and then cheered and broke into the "Old Hundred" anthem as the numbers proved the House had indeed agreed to grant them suffrage. But the fight was not yet won. The Anthony amendment still had to pass the Senate and then be approved by three-quarters of the state legislatures.

For a while, it looked as though the Senate would vote down the measure. President Wilson interceded once more on the behalf of suffrage. In a historic speech before the Senate on September 30, 1918, President Wilson cited the work women were doing in support of World War I and asked the Senate to pass the amendment as "a necessary war measure."[39]

But President Wilson's appeal was not sufficient. With elections just around the corner, the NAWSA sought to replace senators who opposed woman suffrage with pro-suffrage candidates. The NAWSA targeted four states—Delaware, Massachusetts, New Hampshire, and New Jersey—where they might be able to influence the election. Although the women lost in New Hampshire and New Jersey, in Delaware and Massachusetts their campaigns were instrumental in replacing antisuffrage incumbents with men who were in favor of giving women the vote. The strategy worked. On June 4, 1919, the Senate approved the Anthony amendment, sending it on to the states for ratification.

The national leaders of the suffrage movement had succeeded in making suffrage a national issue. Often through trial and error, they had sharpened the tools that would be used to gain the right to vote and had framed the arguments that would be used throughout the decades-long fight for woman suffrage. Pursuing their goals together, just a few women had brought countless women into the movement, spawned and nurtured suffrage organizations on the grassroots level, and provided inspiration for local leaders.

Chapter 3:
Grassroots Organizers: Working at the Local Level

❧

Although much of the historical record of the woman suffrage movement has been devoted to the suffragists who achieved national acclaim, the movement was fueled by and succeeded because of countless women who participated in the struggle behind the scenes in their own neighborhoods and communities. Some of these women joined the state and local suffrage organizations, or ad hoc, informal groups that led petition drives and fund-raising campaigns for the cause. Others simply participated in the discussion, keeping the issue of woman suffrage at the forefront of daily life, encouraging their sisters in the struggle, and persuading their husbands and brothers to vote for the cause in referendum.

Where referenda were held, national organizations such as the NWSA and the AWSA sent organizers. Many locals viewed the national suffrage leaders with suspicion or contempt. Here, grassroots campaigns played a particularly critical role in advancing the cause of suffrage. Local residents recognized best the unique chal-

lenges and arguments suffrage was likely to encounter in a particular area and could often best strategize about how to meet these challenges. In the South, for example, the issue of woman suffrage was tied up with the enfranchisement of African Americans. Southerners also worried that giving women the right to vote would further undermine their genteel, traditional way of life, masculinizing women and disrupting the household. Similarly, women who had been born and raised in the West understood the pioneer mentality and could often relate better to westerners than could women from the East.

Grassroots organizers also brought other constituencies into the movement. College women formed on-campus suffrage organizations, which became increasingly powerful over time. In some areas, organizers tapped newly formed women's labor organizations, giving the movement added momentum and paving the way for change.

The right to vote was finally gained through a constitutional amendment, a process that required ratification by three-quarters of the states. Grassroots organizers played a critical role in galvanizing action to secure its passage. State and local organizations that had continued to focus attention on the state legislature rather than devoting their full attention to the national campaign were best prepared for the ratification campaign. These were the states that were quickest to achieve ratification of the new constitutional amendment.

Organizing for Women's Rights

The first suffragists began to focus on the need for organizing and drawing new proponents into the work, as well as agitating for the vote through petition and argument. On the heels of the first women's rights conventions of the 1850s, women's rights organizations were being formed throughout New England and beyond. By 1873 all of the New England states had woman suffrage associations. And similar organizations were soon formed throughout the Midwest.

Like the attendees of the Seneca Falls Convention, the members of state and local suffrage associations faced ridicule in the press and social disapproval. They were committed to accomplishing what they set out to do, however, and, despite a lack of political experience, quickly began to use the political tools at their disposal. In 1867 Mary Colburn, a longtime women's rights advocate, petitioned the Minnesota state legislature to enfranchise women. The New England Woman Suffrage Association led an 1869 campaign in Massachusetts in which it collected and sent to the state legislature more than seventy-five hundred petitions. And in Toledo, Ohio, Sarah Williams, who later edited a major suffrage journal, and a group of suffragists succeeded in persuading the local library association to permit women to vote and to hold office.

As a result of the efforts of state and local activists, state legislatures began to accept the notion of women's rights legislation. After a long struggle led by Anthony, Stanton, and others, in 1860 the New York state legislature passed a women's rights bill that gave women the right to own property, to file lawsuits, and to share in the custody of children after a divorce. No state went so far as to grant women the right to vote, however.

Campaigning in Kansas

The Kansas legislature passed one of the most progressive women's rights bills of this time. In addition to securing the right to own property and custodianship over children, women in that state were granted the right to vote in school elections. This fell short of the goal that had been set by the Moneka Woman's Rights Society, which had been formed in 1858 to ensure

Clarina Howard Nichols led the fight for suffrage in Kansas. Kansas passed one of the most progressive women's rights bills of the nineteenth century but failed to give women the right to vote.

that women had their rights when Kansas applied for statehood.

Under the leadership of Clarina Howard Nichols, who had moved to Kansas from Vermont, Kansans continued to fight for universal suffrage. In 1867 the Kansas legislature became the first to put the issue of woman suffrage to a vote. Local women and national leaders alike were optimistic about the situation. "The hour of universal freedom is coming for us without violence," wrote Nichols. "Those who have fought the oppressor, and freed the slave and demand suffrage for him, will not forget the women who prayed and wept and wrought for them. . . . We have been on a political equality with the negro too long not to be lifted with him now." [40]

Local Kansans lobbied hard. Nichols donated four weeks to stump throughout the state, "although she was farming at the time and there was no money to pay her," [41] according to Ellen Carol DuBois. Others stayed in their own communities to rally the support of neighbors and friends. "Old Mrs. Dr. Updegraff," for example, the wife of the first speaker of the Kansas legislature, used her considerable connections to further the cause in Osawatomie County. Kansas suffragists held meetings in their parlors and wrote newspaper editorials explaining their reasons for wanting the vote. They also helped organize lecture tours for Lucy Stone and Henry Blackwell, Susan B. Anthony and Elizabeth Cady Stanton, and other suffrage leaders.

Despite constant pressure from local and national suffragists, the referenda for woman suffrage and for African American suffrage both failed to garner the majority votes necessary from men. The failure of the measure dashed the suffragists' hopes to make Kansas "the State of the Future," as Henry Blackwell put it. [42]

Planting the Seeds

Grassroots organizers were busy in other states as well. In many places, women bonded together in loose-knit, self-help societies; these groups became fertile ground for the seeds of suffrage. Long before settling in Utah, for example, Mormon women had organized themselves in relief societies, with the charge of caring for the sick and the poor. "These societies were re-established in Utah, beginning in 1867," write historians Eleanor Flexner and Ellen Fitzpatrick; "they undertook not only the care of the sick and the indigent in the scattered Mormon settlements, but later such planned activities of the Mormon state as the preservation of grain, and the fostering of new industries."[43] The women built on these organizations to turn attention to other issues, including woman suffrage. Emmeline B. Wells, for example, used her role as editor of the Mormon Women's Relief Society's magazine to advocate woman suffrage, as well as educational and economic opportunities. "I believe in women, especially thinking women,"[44] she wrote.

Women throughout the West took time away from their families and farms to campaign on behalf of woman suffrage. Organizing suffrage clubs and lobbying state legislatures was hard work, in most places requiring long journeys from one small town to the next. Despite her responsibilities as sole provider for herself and her family, Oregonian Abigail Scott Duniway traveled continuously to organize women

Abigail Scott Duniway campaigned tirelessly throughout Oregon for suffrage. Women were unable to vote in Oregon until 1912.

in the tiny outposts of Oregon and beyond, sharing the suffrage argument with those who would listen. "She was alone as the women back East, after the Seneca Falls convention, were never alone," write Flexner and Fitzpatrick. "Geography made the problems of arranging conventions and establishing a cohesive organization nearly insuperable, and . . . she traveled literally thousands of miles in all seasons, by stage coach, river boat, and sleigh, to speak wherever a few would gather to hear her."[45]

From 1870 to 1910, seventeen state referenda on woman suffrage were held in eleven states. The states to follow in Kansas's footsteps were Michigan (1874), Colorado (1877), Nebraska (1882), Oregon (1884), and South Dakota (1890). In each case, local women organized campaigns and toiled to convince the male electorate that they should have the vote. The campaigns were typically understaffed and underfunded. Most could not overcome the obstacles of spreading the message in an era of unsophisticated communication and transportation systems, and most failed in the face of the well-organized opposition.

Women Win in the West

But the story was different in Wyoming. Shopkeeper Esther Morris heard Susan B. Anthony speak on behalf of woman suffrage in a tiny outpost in the territory of Wyoming and was moved by her argument. She began to talk to other Wyoming women—and men—about women's rights. The women, and many men, of Wyoming saw little reason that women should not vote. Women had played an influential role in settling the frontier, resulting in a relatively egalitarian view of their roles and abilities. In 1869 the tiny legislature of Wyoming passed a bill granting women the right to vote. Just a few months later, another women's suffrage bill passed in the territory of Utah. Women were also successful in Colorado and Idaho in the 1890s.

These campaigns were won by a combination of strategies undertaken for the most part by local women. In Idaho, for example, Emma Smith DeVoe orchestrated a remarkable campaign. She worked quietly to build a league of two thousand suffragists and won over legislators to put the question of woman suffrage on the ballot. According to *A History of the American Suffragist Movement*, success resulted from a simple grassroots strategy: "Every woman

Women line up to vote in Wyoming in 1869. Many western states granted women the right to vote decades before Congress passed the suffrage amendment.

personally solicited her neighbor, her doctor, her grocer, her laundrywagon driver, the postman and even the man who collected the garbage."[46]

The suffragists recognized that each congressman won over, each vote gained, and each successful state campaign was an arrow in their quiver. Each vote cast by women represented a small bit of influence. They called on the women in the West to exercise their vote to induce politicians to support woman suffrage and to hold them accountable for their stance on women's rights. Although the state-by-state campaigns were slow and tedious, even small successes fueled the woman suffrage movement during the decades to come.

The First Women Cast Their Ballots

After women in Wyoming won the right to vote, others watched carefully to see the impact of woman suffrage on the political and social scene. Some anticipated that woman suffrage would change the results of elections and disrupt the orderly electoral process; others believed that women would vote much as their male counterparts voted and that little would change. The following observation of a New England minister who had just arrived in Wyoming demonstrates the peaceful nature of the transition. This excerpt is from *Century of Struggle* by Eleanor Flexner and Ellen Fitzpatrick.

I saw the rough mountaineers maintaining the most respectful decorum whenever the women approached the polls, and heard the timely warning of one of the leading canvassers as he silenced an incipient quarrel with uplifted finger, saying "Hist! Be quiet! A woman is coming!" And I was compelled to allow that in this new country, supposed at that time to be infested by hordes of cut-throats, gamblers and abandoned characters, I had witnessed a more quiet election than it had been my fortune to see in the quiet towns of Vermont. I saw ladies attended by their husbands, brothers or sweethearts, ride to the place of voting and alight in the midst of a silent crowd, and pass through an open space to the polls, depositing their votes with no more exposure to insult or injury than they would expect on visiting a grocery store or meat market. Indeed, they were much safer here, every man of their party was pledged to shield them, while every member of the other party feared the influence of any signs of disrespect.

Reaching New Constituencies

Grassroots workers were also successful in bringing the issue of woman suffrage to new audiences. As an increasing number of women went on to higher education, college and university campuses became new breeding grounds for political activism. Having been drawn to the movement themselves while students at Radcliffe, Boston suffragists Maud Wood Park and Inez Haynes Crillmore spearheaded the active recruitment of young, educated women to the movement, and the NAWSA began to feature what were known as "College Evenings" at their conventions. In 1908 college suffrage groups from fifteen states came together as the National College Women's Equal Suffrage League. M. Carey Thomas, one of the first women to graduate from Cornell University, declared, "Now women have won the right to higher education and economic independence. The right to become citizens of the state is the next and inevitable consequence of education and work outside the home. We have gone so far; we must go farther. We cannot go back."[47]

In addition to pursuing traditional careers as teachers and nurses, growing numbers of women were becoming doctors, lawyers, and journalists. As women became adept in these professions, arguments about their inferior intellect lost credibility. Mary Putnam Jacobi, the first woman physician to be a member of the New York Academy of Medicine, argued that educational advancement "and the new activities into which [women] have been led by it—in the work of charities, in the professions, and in the direction of public education—naturally and logically tend toward the same result, their political equality."[48]

Suffragists sought to expand their ranks by spreading their message at meetings of literary, civic, church, and charitable organizations. They also joined discussions at parlor meetings—a type of informal gathering that was common among middle-class Victorian women. One suffragist described the role of the parlor meeting:

> You had these little afternoon gatherings of women, maybe six or eight women. You had a cup of tea. A little social gathering. While we were drinking tea, I gave them a little talk and they asked questions about what was going on.... It was alot [sic] better, I thought at the time, than to have a lecture. Because a lot of them wouldn't go to a lecture. And it was what I could do.[49]

The parlor meeting provided a nonintimidating forum for reaching even the most modest Victorian woman who never would have considered attending a public lecture or rally. Professional suffrage speakers would often join these parlor meetings the day before a major suffrage rally in the hope of encouraging some of the women present to take the next step toward suffrage.

Donating Dollars to the Cause

As women gained rights in other areas, they were more able to lend financial support. Some women played a critical role in this area. Wealthy women, including the

Winning State by State

T he state-by-state approach to winning the vote was an arduous process. In Wyoming and Utah, the first states to guarantee woman suffrage, success was achieved through an act of the territorial legislature, rather than referendum. The following excerpt is from "Rethinking Article V: Term Limits and the Seventeenth and Nineteenth Amendments," a 1994 article published in *Yale Law Journal,* written by Kris Kobach, a professor at the University of Missouri, and reprinted at www.law.cornell.edu. In this article, Kobach gives an overview of the successes and failures of woman suffrage advocates in the states.

In virtually every state, the extension of the franchise to women would require the passage of a constitutional amendment, which depended upon winning a majority of the male electorate in a referendum. Over the next fifty-two years [after 1868], the suffragists would wage fifty-six referendum campaigns in twenty-nine different states and territories. Initially, the effort to win the states proceeded slowly and yielded few successes. The first referendum on the subject had already been held in Kansas in 1867, where the suffragists lost. However, this defeat had been balanced in 1869 and 1870 by minor victories in the territories of Wyoming and Utah. In each, the territorial legislature had voted to enfranchise women. Referendums were not required.

The campaign to bring woman suffrage into existence state by state accelerated in the 1880s and 1890s. Between 1882 and 1898, the question was placed on eleven state referendum ballots in nine different states. However, it passed in only two—Colorado in 1893, and Idaho in 1896. Opponents of the suffrage movement found it easy to exploit the fact that many suffragists were also active in the prohibition movement, a connection which aroused the antagonism of the "wets."

At the turn of the century, the state-by-state fight of the suffragists reached its nadir. During the eleven-year period of 1899–1909, proponents of woman suffrage were able to persuade the legislatures of only two states to place the issue on the ballot—once in New Hampshire

Women of the Suffrage Movement

wives of railroad builder Leland Stanford and media mogul William Randolph Hearst, gave substantial sums to support the California campaign for suffrage in 1896. In addition to contributing substantial sums of money, New York socialite Mrs. Clarence McKay organized her own suffrage league and used her wealth and influence to recruit many of New York's most prominent women to join. Alva Smith

(1902) and three times in Oregon (1900, 1906, 1908). In none of these referendums was suffrage approved. The overall strategy, however, was not abandoned. In 1908, Theodore Roosevelt counseled the movement to "Go, get another state." The aging Susan B. Anthony was of the same view:

> "I don't know the exact number of States we shall have to have. . . . but I do know that there will come a day when that number will automatically and resistlessly act on the Congress of the United States to compel the submission of a federal suffrage amendment. And we shall recognize that day when it comes."

The tide was soon to turn in the suffragists' favor. In 1910, they pulled off a surprise victory in a state referendum in Washington. And in 1911, a California legislature under the sway of Progressives in both major parties agreed to submit a state woman suffrage amendment to the voters. It passed by a narrow margin of only 3587 votes.

These two victories had a momentous impact on the rest of the nation. In November 1912, suffrage amendments went before voters in six states, winning in three. Soon, additional states fell into line. In total, during the period from 1910 to 1918, twenty-four states held a total of thirty-one referendums on the question. Of these, eleven states voted for woman suffrage. By the end of 1918, the movement had achieved referendum victories in thirteen states. In addition, the two territories to adopt suffrage had been admitted to the Union, making a total of fifteen states in which women could vote in elections at every level of government. Suffragists anticipated that their moment had come.

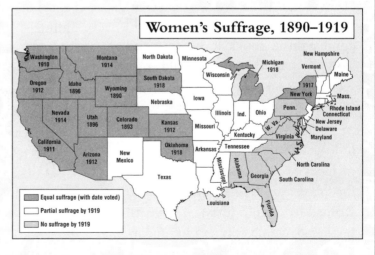

Women's Suffrage, 1890–1919

Belmont, who had married and then divorced an heir to the multimillion-dollar estate of Cornelius Vanderbilt, gave hundreds of thousands of dollars to the cause over the course of her lifetime.

Despite these large donors, suffrage organizations continued to operate on a shoestring budget, and fundraising remained a key activity of these organizations. Speakers from out of town routinely paid their own expenses and sometimes committed funds to the local cause as well. Ida Husted Harper, chair of California's suffrage publicity committee, wrote:

> A large photograph of Miss Anthony and Miss Shaw was given for every $2 pledge, and many poor seamstresses and washerwomen fulfilled their pledges in twenty-five cent installments, coming eight times with their mite. Often when there was not enough money at headquarters to buy a postage stamp, there would come a timid knock at the door and a poorly-dressed woman would enter with a quarter or a half dollar, saying "I have done without tea this week to bring you this money;" or a poor little clerk would say "I made a piece of fancy work evenings and sold it for this dollar." Many a woman who worked hard ten hours a day to earn her bread, would come to headquarters and carry home a great armload of circulars to fold and address that night. And there were teachers and stenographers and other working women who went without a winter coat to give money to this movement for freedom. [50]

Harper's account reveals the breadth of the movement at the turn of the century, as the movement attracted both very wealthy and working-class women. Working women—particularly those who were working in the garment sector and other industries—were becoming experienced in organizing. Frustrated by the deplorable conditions and lack of power, women in the garment industry called strikes and demanded reforms. The NAWSA recognized the potential of these women to aid their cause. A 1907 article in its newsletter proclaimed, "We realize that probably it will not be the educated workers, the college women, the men's association for equal suffrage, but the people who are fighting for industrial freedom who will be our vital force at the finish." [51] Working women became particularly instrumental in New England and New York, where their large numbers and organizing experience made them a formidable force.

Suffrage in the South

If woman suffrage was hard-won in the North and West, it faced seemingly insurmountable odds in the South, where traditional values were more deeply held. Most southerners looked on woman suffrage as an outrage, born of the abolitionist movement. Yet, there were women in the southern states who toiled relentlessly on behalf of the cause, even while making little headway.

Yet, woman suffrage took on a different tenor in the South than in other regions of the country. As the argument took hold in the late nineteenth century, advocates focused on the fact that the enfranchisement of women could be achieved without extending the right to vote to *black* women. Thus, southerners argued, woman suffrage could in fact help bolster white supremacy.

Southern women often continued their other activities while advocating suffrage. Belle Kearney of Mississippi, for example, promoted suffrage along with

Two women picket during the Ladies Tailors strike of 1910. Working women became a powerful force in the suffrage movement in the East.

Lobbying at the Local Level

Although the fight for a constitutional amendment was spearheaded by those in Washington, D.C., women across the country met with their congressmen to lobby them to support the legislation. In the following excerpt from *Century of Struggle* by Eleanor Flexner and Ellen Fitzpatrick, a Wisconsin suffragist describes her work.

I was frightfully tired from my work when I returned from [the December 1917 Washington NAWSA convention] but I started right in to secure the vote of Mr. Davidson of this district and of Mr. Classon of the Ninth District.* I traveled over a good deal of their districts not making public speeches but seeing men who were politically prominent and talking the question out with each one of them, putting my best efforts into making them see the situation from our viewpoint. Some days I got up at 5:30, took an electric train, and did not get home until midnight, talking the question out with from six to eight men and going from office to office all during the day. The day I was in Appleton it was ten below. The day I was in Marinette there was a very bad snow storm. I spent the night there and got to Oconto before any of the walks were clean, so had to wade through snow up to the tops of my shoes. There are no street cars in Oconto. As far as I could see there were no taxis. I worked up until the last moment, until I knew nothing more could reach Washington, and then I gave it up. There is nothing the matter with me except nervous and physical exhaustion. I am not complaining because I would do it all over again to get the result even if I were in bed for six months.

* Both men voted for the amendment.

temperance in her role as a professional lecturer for the WCTU. As these women formed state organizations for women's rights and suffrage throughout the South, they forged bonds with one another—bonds that would be instrumental in the ratification struggle soon to unfold in the United States and to conclude with a bitter struggle in Tennessee.

Even more than in other regions of the country, the suffrage leaders in the South were well-known to one another. Historian Marjorie Spruill Wheeler writes, "[They] relied heavily on each other for advice on organization and strategy, assisted one another as lecturers and lobbyists, and provided greatly needed moral support for one another as they fought for years against great odds and with so little success."[52]

Some southern suffragists, including Laura Clay of Kentucky and Kate Gordon of Louisiana, became active in the national movement as well. However, like their sisters, they considered themselves southerners first and foremost. These women wanted to win suffrage at home, in the states in which they lived. Mary Johnston, a leading suffragist in Virginia, wrote in 1905, "Virginia (and incidentally the entire South) is my country, and not the stars and stripes but the stars and bars is my flag."[53]

Even the staunchest suffragists in the South focused on earning the right to vote through the state legislature. Most opposed an amendment to the U.S. Constitution, arguing that such an act would undermine the power of state governments—a right they wanted to wield to keep African Americans from voting. Despite devoting years of their lives to lobbying and organizing on behalf of the cause, both Clay and Gordon opposed the amendment during the ratification process.

The Battle for Ratification

In 1918 the endless lobbying and petitioning of suffragists on the national, state, and local levels succeeded in convincing enough congressmen to vote for the Anthony amendment to send it on to the states for ratification.

States where suffrage had already been won sometimes had to reorganize, but women in states that had been working for suffrage right up to the adoption of the amendment simply turned their attention to ratification. In Wisconsin, for example, suffragists had continued their work organizing, raising money, and lobbying the legislature. As a result, on June 9, Wisconsin, which had not received suffrage for women prior to the amendment, became the first state to ratify the amendment. (Michigan and Illinois ratified the amendment later the same day.)

Many of the ratification campaigns were difficult even in states where passage seemed assured, but the suffragists did not back down. In states where the legislature was still in session, women tallied votes and worked to secure pledges from state legislators to ratify. In states where the legislature had already adjourned, they put pressure on the governor to call a special session.

Many women dedicated months to the cause. The following account of women in Vermont who converged on the capital to convince the governor to form a ratification committee exemplifies the dedication of women, many of whom had not been at the forefront of the movement until now.

Twelve of the fourteen counties were represented by four hundred women who went to the State Capitol, overcoming the obstacles of long distances, almost impassable roads, and poor train service. Many came from towns remote from railroads, one woman walking five miles to the station. Others ploughed through deep snow and over [muddy] and rocky roads before daylight. Reaching the Capitol they marched, a silent army of loyal soldiers, through a cold drenching rain and took their places before the Governor's chair. One by one, in a sentence or two, they presented Vermont's case. [54]

A woman in Oklahoma even gave up her life. Suffering from influenza, Aloysius Lark-Miller, the secretary of the Oklahoma women's ratification committee, ignored her doctor's orders and delivered her address to a county convention as scheduled. She died two days later.

"Armageddon in Tennessee"

By the summer of 1920, thirty-five states had ratified the amendment; just one more was needed. When the Delaware legislature unexpectedly defeated the amendment in June, the suffragists set their sights on Tennessee. Historian Anastatia Sims sets the stage for what she calls "Armageddon in Tennessee":

During a steamy southern summer, Nashville, the "Athens of the South," became the site of one of the most fiercely fought contests in American political history. For the amend-ment's friends and foes alike it was Armageddon—the final battle in the long, bitter struggle that had, in the words of one observer, pitted "powers that pray" against "powers that prey." [55]

Suffragists initiated a campaign to organize support. Carrie Chapman Catt helped coordinate the venture, first from her home in New York and then from a hotel in Nashville. She instructed Tennessee suffragists to poll the legislators to learn how they were planning to vote on the suffrage amendment. She told supporters to get the commitment of legislators, but not to count on them not changing their minds. Catt arrived in Nashville in July with clothes to last for a few days. She ended up staying for over a month as she organized to counter the vociferous opposition.

To counter antisuffragist claims, the suffragists organized massive publicity campaigns and speeches. They demonstrated how suffrage would enable women to fulfill their domestic responsibilities more effectively. To appease southerners, they pledged to uphold white supremacy and argued that the measures that disenfranchised African American men could be used to disenfranchise African American women.

Success at Last!

As the legislature convened to vote on suffrage on August 9, both sides tried any means possible to sway the politicians to

Alice Paul drapes a flag over the National Women's Party headquarters in Washington, D.C., to celebrate ratification of the Nineteenth Amendment. In 1920 Tennessee became the thirty-sixth and deciding state to ratify the amendment.

vote for their side. "Automobile rides, hugs, kisses, even the absurdity of powdering the members' noses and rouging their cheeks in the assembly hall were frequently witnessed,"[56] reported a Chattanooga paper.

As suffrage was debated over the next several days, suffragists patrolled the hotel and train and bus stations to keep legislators who had pledged their support from leaving before the final vote was taken. On August 18, the Tennessee House voted. As in Congress months before, some of the men made heroic efforts to cast their votes. One delegate left the hospital against his doctor's advice; another chose to vote rather than to be with his dying baby. The tally, 48 to 48, spelled defeat for women, when Harry Burns changed his vote.

Remembering his mother's plea to vote for ratification, the twenty-four-year-old voted for the affirmative. Countering attacks that he had been bribed, Burns declared for the record: "I changed my vote in favor of ratification because I believe in full suffrage as a right; I believe we had a moral and legal right to ratify; I know that a mother's advice is always safest for her boy to follow and my mother wanted me to vote for ratification." [57]

That night, Catt sent a telegram to North Carolina suffragist Gertrude Weil: "The thirty-sixth state is won." [58]

Victory had not come easily. State legislatures had considered the issue hundreds of times. There had been fifty-six statewide referenda to male voters and forty-seven attempts to add suffrage amendments to state constitutions. Literally millions of women—and men—had dedicated themselves to the cause.

Chapter 4:
Militant Suffragists

From the beginning of the woman suffrage movement, there were women who were willing to cross the lines of acceptable behavior to adopt methods that others perceived as confrontational or militant. In the mid-1800s, simply showing up at a polling place to register was considered militant. By the dawn of the twentieth century, however, tactics had become increasingly confrontational and more extreme. By the late stage of the movement, women were calling attention to their plight by any means necessary. In addition to the suffrage rallies and parades that had become a common tactic of the movement, women suffragists—or suffragettes, as members of the more radical faction of the movement were called—picketed the White House. When they were arrested, they responded with even more extreme forms of protest, such as publicized hunger strikes. The introduction of militant tactics changed the landscape of the suffrage battlefield. The fight for suffrage moved beyond the realm of legislatures into the hearts and minds of the public.

Early Dissenters

When Elizabeth Cady Stanton included woman suffrage in her demands at the Seneca Falls Convention, she shocked many of those in attendance. Yet, even at that early stage, there were some women who agreed that suffrage was their right as property owners, if not as citizens of the United States. Denied the vote, some women engaged in brave protests against the laws of the day.

In 1859 Mary Harrington, a property owner in Claremont, New Hampshire, refused to pay her taxes. Arguing that there could be no taxation without representation, she said that she was not represented because she could not vote. The tax collector seized her furniture as payment nevertheless. Ellen Carol DuBois writes, "Other local activists, more than we may ever know launched their own protests, but often the woman's rights movement was too small and weak to sustain them."[59] Like Harrington, the women who rebelled against their plight had no recourse and little encouragement when they failed in their attempts to be heard.

Women Head to the Polls

As women organized, they found strength in numbers. In the decades following the Civil War, women became increasingly impatient with the gradual gains they were making. Some women believed that rather than ask for the vote, they should demand it as their right as citizens. Victoria Woodhull, an outspoken radical who became well known as the publisher of *Woodhull and Claflin's Weekly,* proposed to Congress that under the Fourteenth and Fifteenth Amendments women were already enfranchised. "With the right to vote sex has nothing to do," she argued before the Judiciary Committee of the House of Representatives in 1871. "All people of both sexes have the right to vote, unless prohibited by special limiting terms less comprehensive than race or color. No such limiting terms exist in the Constitution."[60] The Judiciary Committee issued a favorable report on woman suffrage, but the measure went no further.

Victoria Woodhull speaks at a public rally. In 1871 Woodhull persuaded the House Judiciary Committee that the constitutional right to vote did not discriminate by sex.

Meanwhile, an increasing number of women were becoming bold enough to go to the polls to argue their case directly to local elections officials. In 1868, in Vineland, New Jersey, 172 women (four of them African American) cast their votes for president. They were barred from casting their votes with men, however, and had to use a separate ballot box. In the end, election officials refused to include their votes in the count, but women in Vineland continued to cast their votes in this way for several years. Similarly, in the 1870 election, Angelina Grimké Weld and Sara Grimké, who was now almost eighty years of age, led forty women through a driving snowstorm in Hyde Park, Massachusetts, to cast their votes in a separate box.

Emboldened by the Enforcement Act of 1870, which sought to strengthen the provisions of the Fifteenth Amendment, hundreds of women in towns across America tried to register and cast their votes. Going to the polls to demand the vote was a bold step; women sought courage by joining together. Mary Olney Brown, a pioneer in the Washington Territory, recalled later:

I wrote to some prominent women . . . urging them to go out and vote. But . . . I was looked upon as a fanatic, and the idea of women voting was regarded as an absurdity. . . . Knowing that if anything was [to be] done

someone must take the initiative, I determined to cast aside my timidity. . . . I [went to] the polling place, accompanied by my husband, my daughter, and her husband—a little band of four—looked upon with pity and contempt.[61]

Despite Brown's impassioned arguments, the election officials in her ward refused to allow her to vote.

A few daring women were more successful than Brown had been. Election officials tended to make decisions on a case-by-case basis. In 1871, when Catherine Stebbins, who had helped draft the Declaration of Sentiments at the Seneca Falls Convention, and Nanette Gardener attempted to register in their Detroit district, election officials turned away Stebbins but allowed Gardener to register. Their reasoning was that Stebbins was married and thus represented politically by her husband, but Gardener, a widow, would otherwise have no representation. Gardener voted in the 1871 election and in several elections in subsequent years.

The Arrest of the Most Famous Suffragist

The most famous of the women who headed to the polls in 1872 was Susan B. Anthony. She succeeded in convincing the men at a polling station in Rochester, New York, to allow her to register, but when she

During the 1872 election, Susan B. Anthony was arrested for attempting to vote. Anthony was found guilty, but she refused to pay the fine.

and fifteen other women arrived at the polls, they were turned away. When word spread that Anthony and several other women had tried to vote in the national election, government officials arrested her for "knowingly, wrongfully and unlawfully vot[ing] for a representative to the Congress of the United States."[62] The election officials who had allowed her to register were also arrested.

At her trial, Anthony was prohibited from speaking in her own defense because laws did not allow women to testify in a court of law. The judge found her guilty and fined her one hundred dollars—a fine she steadfastly refused to pay.

By this time, Susan B. Anthony was famous. Newspapers nationwide considered the suit brought against her and her response newsworthy. Anthony had not gained the right to vote, but she had gained significant publicity for her cause.

Taking the Suffrage Issue to Court

Some of the women who were turned away by election officials took their case to court under the Enforcement Act. Ellen Rand Van Valkenberg brought suit against election officials of Santa Cruz, California, becoming the first woman to do so. Virginia Minor took her case all the way to the Supreme Court after the election officials in St. Louis refused to register her and a group of fellow suffragists. Denied the right to sue because she was a woman, Virginia Minor arranged for her husband Francis, who was a lawyer, to try her case for her.

These women were unsuccessful in convincing the courts that the U.S. Constitution guaranteed their right to vote. In *Minor v. Happersett* (1874), the Supreme Court ruled unanimously that citizenship meant "membership in a nation and noth-

ing more" and that "the Constitution of the United States does not confer the right of suffrage upon any one." Voting eligibility was decided by the states, the Court declared, and changes to voting laws must happen as a result of explicit legislation or constitutional amendment. "If the law is wrong it ought to be changed," the justices wrote, "but the power for that is not with us." [63]

New and Controversial Tactics

Other women were coming into the movement with new ideas and strategies. Among these was Harriot Stanton Blatch, the daughter of Elizabeth Cady Stanton. In 1907 Blatch set up the Equality League of Self-Supporting Women, a New York organization for working women that had suffrage as a main objective. In 1910 this organization changed its name to the Woman's Political Union (WPU). Within a year, the WPU had over nineteen thousand members, many of them drawn from the ranks of working women.

Blatch set out to utilize the new tool at her disposal. At her request, Clara Silver and Mary Duffy, workers in the garment industry, testified before the New York legislature on behalf of woman suffrage— becoming the first working-class women to put forth arguments before a legislative body. They explained how disfranchisement contributed to their difficult working conditions. "To be left out by the State just sets up a prejudice against us," Silver

Register Now!

In 1872 national woman suffrage leaders urged their colleagues to go out and vote. In some places, newspaper editorials, such as the one that follows, urged women to action. The confrontational tone of this editorial of November 1, 1872, published in a local newspaper in Rochester, New York, is credited with prompting Susan B. Anthony to register to vote.

Now Register? To-day and to-morrow are the only remaining opportunities. If you were not permitted to vote, you would fight for the right, undergo all privations for it, face death for it. You have it now at the cost of five minutes' time to be spent in seeking your place of registration, and having your name entered. And yet, on election day, less than a week hence, hundreds of you are likely to lose your votes because you have not thought it worth while to give the five minutes. To-day and to-morrow are your only opportunieis. Register now!

testified. "Bosses think and women come to think themselves that [we] don't count for so much as men." [64]

Harriot Stanton Blatch introduced other new, more aggressive tactics. She had spent time in England, where a radical woman suffrage movement was afoot. Blatch believed that the American woman suffrage movement suffered from a lack of publicity and thought that some of the English tactics might remedy this situation. She organized open-air meetings and held the first major woman suffrage parade in the United States.

Alice Paul and the Congressional Committee

Several other American women who had been to England and taken part in the suffrage movement there began to organize similar campaigns in the United States. Some of the English movement's leaders visited the United States. But it was Alice Paul who soon became the militant movement's most formidable leader. Like Blatch, Paul had spent time in England, where she became familiar with the militant tactics of the British suffragettes. Upon returning home in 1910, Paul set about motivating the women in the United States to be more vehement in their demands for suffrage.

In 1912, under the auspices of the NAWSA, Paul established the new Congressional Committee, an organization based in Washington to take on lobbying Congress for a constitutional amendment. With Alice Paul as chairman, the Congressional Committee (which became the Congressional Union late in 1913) was composed of Lucy Burns, Mary Beard, Dora Lewis, and Crystal Eastman. All of these women lived in New York or Washington, and all were, says historian Doris Weatherford, "young, educated, and worldly." [65] Under Paul's leadership, they ushered in a new era of what historian Linda Ford calls "an aggressive, unapologetically egalitarian, militant style" [66] modeled after the English woman suffrage movement.

Most citizens—even some of those who believed in woman suffrage—were appalled by such so-called unladylike antics. When the tactics proved too radical for the NAWSA, Paul and the other militant leaders broke from the NAWSA and formed the National Woman's Party (NWP), into which the Congressional Union was folded in 1916.

"Spectacle and Street Theater"

With the aim of focusing attention on the woman suffrage movement through virtually any means, militant women staged suffrage parades in many cities. The parades were huge, carefully choreographed events with floats, women on horseback, and music. In a 1910 parade, ninety automobiles (still a novelty) took part. Edith Mayo writes, "The NWP parades and demon-

The English Suffrage Movement

Many of the militant ideas the American suffragists used at the turn of the century were borrowed from their counterparts in England. Harriot Stanton Blatch and Alice Paul had both spent time in England before returning to become leaders in the American woman suffrage movement. In the following excerpt from Doris Stevens's *Jailed for Freedom,* editor Carol O'Hare explains the tactics of the English militant suffrage movement that militant American women took as models.

In 1903 Emmeline Pankhurst and her daughters Christabel and Sylvia founded the Women's Social and Political Union (WSPU) in England. Its objective was to be independent of any political party and to persuade the public to vote against any parliamentary candidate who did not support votes for women. Although other woman suffrage organizations had long existed, the WSPU was the first and largest militant group. It drew much of its early support from working women.

The suffragettes, as they were called, sought new methods to achieve political equality: demonstration, confrontation and peaceful agitation at first and, later, more radical tactics. When the women were arrested for their activities, they chose prison over paying fines, went on hunger strikes and endured forced feeding. They suffered appalling physical hardship, beatings, and other brutal treatment. Over one thousand members of the WSPU were eventually imprisoned. Emmeline Pankhurst nearly died from numerous hunger strikes. . . .

The WSPU's challenge to the government lasted until 1914 when England became involved in World War I. Partial suffrage was granted to women in 1918; universal women's suffrage came ten years later.

strations . . . were carefully planned to surprise, educate, and engage the public and the press. Paul created a series of themes and special events, and each action had a particular objective. As political theater, they were never repetitive, boring, or predictable." [67]

The suffragists often dressed in white, topped by elaborate headwear that became known as "the suffrage hat." The white sea of marchers was contrasted by their colorful ribbons, banners, and flags.

Several of the bigger parades were led by Inez Milholland, a New York suffragist

Alice Paul

Best known for her militant tactics, Alice Paul played a key role in capturing the attention of the American public. The following description of her life and contributions to the woman suffrage movement by editor Carol O'Hare appears in Doris Stevens's *Jailed for Freedom*.

The moment Alice Paul first encountered the militant English suffrage movement, securing rights for women became her passion. Her progressive ideas and belief in equality for women had their origin in her well-to-do Quaker family in New Jersey, and after graduating from Swarthmore College in 1905, she became a social worker in New York City. But when she went to England two years later to continue her studies, she instantly felt an affinity for the revolutionary suffrage campaign being waged under the leadership of the Pankhurst women. . . .

Alice Paul was an extraordinary leader, ingenious fundraiser, and brilliant politician. Her entire life revolved around suffrage. She lived in a cold room so she "would not be tempted to sit up late and read novels." Sometimes she went months without bothering to remove her hat. She expected those around her to dedicate themselves totally to suffrage, but she drove no one harder than she drove herself.

After ratification of the Nineteenth Amendment in 1920, Paul earned three law degrees. Then in 1923 at a convention of the National Woman's Party, she proposed the Equal Rights Amendment (ERA), which stipulated that no right shall be denied or abridged by either the federal government or the states on account of sex. She devoted the rest of her life to this new cause. The ERA finally passed Congress in 1972, but it was never ratified by enough states to become part of the Constitution.

Alice Paul toasts the success of the suffrage movement. A militant leader, Paul lobbied Congress, staged parades, and in 1923 introduced the first Equal Rights Amendment.

Inez Milholland leads a parade promoting woman suffrage through the streets of New York in 1913. Parades and rallies attracted the attention of the press, which had been ignoring the suffrage movement.

known for her pacifist and socialist politics. In 1913 she led a suffrage parade in Washington, D.C., dressed in white and perched upon a horse, becoming, historian Edith Mayo writes, "fixed firmly in American suffrage imagery as the breathtaking figure of the herald. . . . Militant, yet godly, the figure represented moral authority and suggested martyrdom for a righteous cause, both strong themes in the NWP's ideology."[68] Milholland became a martyr for the cause when she collapsed during a suffrage speech in Los Angeles in October 1916 and died of pernicious anemia ten days later.

The suffrage parades and open-air rallies accomplished their objective. Until this time, most newspapers declined to carry news or editorials about woman suffrage, but the newspapers now teemed with stories about the women marchers. The militant suffragists deliberately flew in the face of convention, balking at what was considered ladylike behavior. Dubois writes, "Militant tactics broke through the 'press boycott' by violating standards of respectable femininity, making the cause newsworthy, and embracing the subsequent ridicule and attention."[69] Getting attention through any means necessary was a conscious strategy. The *American Suffragette,* published by the NWP, proclaimed: "We . . . believe in standing on street corners and fighting our way to recognition, forcing men to think about us. We glory . . . that we are theatrical."[70]

The suffragists recognized that the best way to get publicity was to go to where there was already national attention. Thus, they decided to hold a parade during Woodrow Wilson's presidential inauguration in Washington, D.C. Organized by Alice Paul, whom historian Edith Mayo calls a "master of spectacle and street theater,"[71] the 1913 parade got more attention than even she expected. The marchers—over eight thousand strong—were grouped into units, each with their own costumes and banners. The path of the parade went up Pennsylvania Avenue, right through the heart of the city and past the U.S. Congress.

As the suffragists marched, some spectators became unruly. Cheers turned to jeers. Men lining the street began to taunt and shove the women. One Baltimore newspaper described the scene:

Eight thousand women, marching in the woman suffrage pageant today, practically fought their way foot by foot up Pennsylvania Avenue, through a surging throng that completely defied Washington police, swamped the marchers, and broke their proces-

sion into little companies. The women, trudging stoutly along under great difficulties, were able to complete their march only when troops of cavalry from Fort Myers were rushed into Washington to take charge of Pennsylvania Avenue. No inauguration has ever produced such scenes, which in many instances amounted to nothing less than riots.[72]

The event was covered in newspapers from coast to coast. Readers were scandalized by the treatment of the women marchers. The police were criticized for their inability or unwillingness to stop the hecklers. Many people who had before opposed suffrage began to reconsider their opinions. The suffragettes had achieved their goal.

To capitalize on their momentum, the suffragettes began "suffrage schools" to educate women on the issue and, according to Paul, held "an uninterrupted series of indoor and outdoor meetings, numbering frequently from five to ten a day."[73] Some of these included plays or other performances that drew crowds who did not consider themselves suffragists and were not interested in politics. And they continued to capture the attention of the press with suffrage parades and rallies.

The suffragettes added dramatic flair also to the process of petitioning Congress. The NWP organized cross-country peti-

Women of the Suffrage Movement

tion drives in which women collected votes while traveling in automobiles. In 1915, for example, Mabel Vernon, Sarah Bard Field, and others traveled across the nation by automobile, carrying over five hundred thousand signatures on a petition for woman suffrage from California to Washington, D.C. Since cars were still rare, people watched in awe as the suffragists drove by. In some rural areas, people had never before seen a car; in most places, it was astonishing to see a woman in the driver's seat. The press also took notice as they passed.

On Parade

Woman suffrage parades proved to be an effective way to gain publicity for the cause. By the 1910s, the suffrage movement had attracted women from all walks of life, as described in the following excerpt from a story in the *New York Times* covering a 1912 march. A lengthier excerpt of this article is included in *Forward into Light,* edited by Madeleine Meyers.

Ten thousand strong, the army of those who believe in the cause of woman's suffrage marched up Fifth Avenue at sundown yesterday in a parade the like of which New York never knew before. . . .

It was a parade of contrasts—contrasts among women. There were women of every occupation and profession, and women of all ages, from those so advanced in years that they had to ride in carriages down to suffragettes so small that they were pushed along in perambulators [baby carriages]. There were women whose faces bore traces of a life of hard work and many worries. There were young girls, lovely of face and fashionably gowned. There were motherly looking women, and others with the confident bearing obtained from contact with the business world.

There were women who smiled in a preoccupied way as though they had just put the roast into the oven, whipped off their aprons and hurried out to be in the parade. They were plainly worried at leaving their household cares for so long, yet they were determined to show their loyalty to the cause. There were women who marched those weary miles who had large bank accounts. There were slender girls, tired after long hours of factory work. There were nurses, teachers, cooks, writers, social workers, librarians, school girls, laundry workers. There were women who work with their heads, and women who work with their hands, and women who never work at all. And they all marched for suffrage.

The Silent Sentinels

In addition to generating publicity for their cause, the militant suffragists declared their intention to hold the party in power—the Democrats—responsible for failing to pass a suffrage amendment. In a convention held in Washington, D.C., Lucy Burns, vice chairman of the Congressional Union, declared: "We ask the Democrats to take action now. Inaction establishes just as clear a record as does a policy of open hostility."[74] Suffragists began interrupting the speeches of President Wilson and other political leaders with pointed questions about women's rights and suffrage and soon were engaging in more openly defiant acts.

In January 1917 the suffragists tried out a new tactic—picketing the White House (the first citizens in American history ever to do so). These so-called Silent Sentinels appeared day after day (except for Sundays), carrying banners sporting political slogans and suffrage demands. In all, as

Suffragettes march around the White House in a silent plea for equal rights in 1917. Suffragettes were the first group to picket the White House.

Women of the Suffrage Movement

many as one thousand women of all ages, races, and religions, from all walks of life and every state of the Union, endured inclement weather and harassment from passersby to demonstrate their commitment to suffrage with their feet.

Like the militants' other tactics, picketing the White House got the attention of the press and the public. In *Jailed for Freedom,* Doris Stevens recalls:

Soon the pickets were the subject of animated conversation in practically every part of the nation. The press cartoonists, by their friendly and satirical comments, helped a great deal in popularizing the campaign. . . . People who had never before thought of suffrage for women had to think of it. . . . People who had thought a little about suffrage were compelled to think more about it. People who had believed in suffrage all their lives, but had never done a stroke of work for it, began to make speeches about it. [75]

Arrest and Imprisonment

On July 14, 1917, after six months of picketing, the suffragettes faced police action. As they marched to the White House gates, they were arrested. Sixteen women were brought to trial. In court, the women defendants rejected the claim that they had broken any laws and refused to be intimidated. Doris Stevens said to the judge,

"This outrageous policy of stupid and brutal punishment will not dampen the ardor of the women. Where sixteen of us face your judgment today there will be sixty tomorrow, so great will be the indignation of our colleagues in this fight." [76]

At the end of the trial, which lasted less than two days, the judge returned a guilty verdict and sentenced the leaders of the picketers to a twenty-five-dollar fine or sixty days in the workhouse. The women refused to pay the fine on the grounds that they were not guilty. When President Wilson learned that the women had begun work at the Occoquan, Virginia, workhouse, he issued a pardon.

The picketers continued their vigilant watch at the gates of the White House. Their numbers grew, and they faced increasing harassment from police and onlookers. In August, one confrontation escalated to a near riot. The police responded by making arrests. At first, the picketers were dismissed, but over time the punishment meted out became harsher. In just a few months, more than two hundred picketers were arrested; almost half of them were found guilty of obstructing traffic or other minor offenses and sentenced to terms at the Occoquan workhouse or District of Columbia jail. Some of the women were sentenced to jail for as long as six months.

The women who were arrested included Alice Paul, Lucy Burns, and other militant leaders. They included in their ranks well-established women in various professions, such as Lavinia Dock, who had earned international renown for her work as a nurse. Some of the women were wealthy; others were married to powerful men. There were several young college graduates, but there were also women of advanced age. Mary Nolan, for example, was seventy-three when she was sentenced to the Occoquan workhouse; Lavinia Dock was sixty.

The suffragettes demanded to be treated as political prisoners, claiming that they were arrested not because they had broken any laws but because of their beliefs. The prisoners were treated with harsh disdain and disregard. Mary Nolan, who was imprisoned in November 1914, described the scene in the workhouse after several of the women were sent to "punishment cells":

We were so terrified we kept very still. . . . Mrs. Cosu was desperately ill as the night wore on. She had a bad heart attack, and then vomiting. We called and called. We asked them to send our doctor because we thought she was dying; there was a woman guard and a man in the corridor, but they paid no attention. A cold wind blew in on us from the outside, and we all lay there shivering and only half conscious until early morning. [77]

Led by Lucy Burns, some women objected to the unfair and harsh treatment by going on a hunger strike. Burns refused to eat for nineteen days, during which the guards subjected her to forced feeding.

As newspapers across the country reported the harsh treatment of the women and the horror of forced feeding, public opinion began to turn. To save embarrassment, the Wilson administration ordered that the women be pardoned and released from prison. Once released, the women dressed in prison garb and went on a speaking tour throughout the country on a train they called the "Prison Special."

The Triumph of Militant Tactics

Although they were sometimes shunned by the mainstream woman suffrage movement, the militants played a critical role in achieving the goal of suffrage. As they moved from one dramatic action to the next, they kept the issue of woman suffrage before the public and put pressure on the politicians. With each act of overt defiance, the militants called attention to their cause. Furthermore, they forced the government to respond, causing many to see the fight as between a group of committed women and a seemingly uncaring, faceless government. The courage and determination of the women fighting for suffrage won admiration and sympathy among citizens—both male and female.

Chapter 5:
African American Women in the Suffrage Movement

❧

Woman suffrage has often been considered a campaign spearheaded by middle-class white women, but this portrayal is incomplete. African Americans were among the many other groups that played a critical role from the beginning—even before the abolition of slavery. Although their words were rarely recorded in the annals of history, African American women often worked hand in hand with white women to form associations and organize women's conferences around the issue of woman suffrage.

Rosalyn Terborg-Penn, a historian and preeminent scholar on the contributions of African Americans to the suffrage movement, writes that there were two primary reasons for the involvement of black women in the suffrage movement:

> At mid-[nineteenth] century their argument was based upon the belief, which was also held by white woman suffragists, that women were second-class citizens who needed the vote to improve their status in society. However, by the late nineteenth

and early twentieth centuries, the rationale had grown to include the argument that black women needed the vote in order to help uplift the race and to obtain their own rights.[78]

Achieving their goals was not easy, however. In the woman suffrage movement—as in all areas of their lives—African American women faced racism. Some woman suffrage organizations barred blacks from membership or refused to let them speak. As a result, African Americans sometimes formed their own parallel organizations, working together to improve their conditions both as blacks and as women.

Antislavery Advocates Take the Lead

Before the Civil War, most of the African Americans living in the United States were slaves. Only the relatively few legally free black women could even think about the possibility of voting. Most of these women lived in northern states where slavery had been outlawed. By the 1830s, free blacks in the North had organized to oppose slavery and promote racial advancement. It was from these groups that women brave enough to speak out came.

Maria Stewart, a free black woman living in Boston, was perhaps the first African American woman to ignore the social convention against women speaking in public. As early as 1830—even before the Grimké sisters—Stewart took to the podium to speak out against slavery and to advocate formal education for girls. She was met with scorn and ridicule, and soon discontinued her public appearances. "I find it is no use for me, as an individual, to try to make myself useful among my color in this city," she said in a farewell address in 1833. "I have made myself contemptible in the eyes of many." [79]

As women joined the abolition movement, they recognized that in order to achieve their goals, they would need to break free of the traditions that bound women. In some cases, African American women worked alongside the white women of the abolition movement. For example, sisters Harriet Forten Purvis and Margaretta Forten, daughters of a wealthy reformer in Philadelphia, were among the women who helped found the Philadelphia Female Anti-Slavery Society. Purvis and Forten also played an instrumental role in planning the first National Women's Rights Convention, which was held in 1854.

Although born a slave and unable to read or write, Sojourner Truth became a powerful speaker on women's rights.

"Ain't I a Woman?"

Sojourner Truth is perhaps the best-known African American suffragist of the early movement. Born Isabella, a slave in a small town in Upstate New York, she was freed when that state outlawed slavery in 1828. After changing her name in 1843, she began traveling through the eastern United States, first preaching the word of God and then lecturing on behalf of the abolition movement. She supported herself in part through sales of *The Narrative of Sojourner Truth,* an account of her life as a slave that was written by Olive Gilbert and published in 1850. After attending the

Women's Rights Convention in Worcester, Massachusetts, Truth committed herself to the cause of suffrage and became a speaker on women's rights issues.

Truth never learned to read or write, but she electrified her audiences with her ardent argument and folksy manner. At a convention held in Akron, Ohio, in 1851,

"A'n't I a Woman?"

N ot everyone thought it was a good idea to allow Sojourner Truth to take the podium at the 1851 women's rights convention in Akron, Ohio. Frances Gage, who presided over the meeting, later wrote that several people thought she should try to stop Truth. But Truth's brief address brought a halt to a heckler's claim that women were too weak-minded to speak. The excerpt here is from Frances Gage's recollections, reprinted in *The Concise History of Woman Suffrage* by Mary J. Buhle and Paul Buhle.

"Dat man ober dar say dat womin needs to be helped into carriages, and lifted ober ditches, and to hab de best place everywhar. Nobody eber helps me into carriages, or ober mud-puddles, or gibs me any best place!" And raising herself to her full height, and her voice to a pitch like rolling thunders, she asked "And a'n't I a woman? Look at me! Look at my arm! (and she bared her right arm to the shoulder, showing her tremendous muscular power). I have ploughed, and planted, and gathered into barns, and no man could head me! And a'n't I a woman? I could work as much and eat as much as a man—when I could get it—and bear de

lash as well! And a'n't I a woman? I have borne thirteen chilern, and seen 'em mos' all sold off to slavery, and when I cried out with my mother's grief, none but Jesus heard me! And a'n't I a woman? . . ."

Turning again to another objector, she took up the defense of Mother Eve. I can not follow her through it all. It was pointed, and witty, and solemn; eliciting at almost every sentence deafening applause; and she ended by asserting? "If de fust woman God ever made was strong enough to turn de world upside down all alone, dese women togedder (and she glanced her eye over the platform) ought to be able to turn it back, and get it right side up again! And now dey is asking to do it, de men better let 'em." Long-continued cheering greeted this. "Bleeged to ye for hearin' on me, and now old Sojourner han't got nothin' more to say."

Amid roars of applause, she returned to her corner, leaving more than one of us with streaming eyes, and hearts beating with gratitude. She had taken us up in her strong arms and carried us safely over the slough of difficulty turning the whole tide in our favor.

Truth took a bold stand, taking the podium to defend women against a clergyman's claim that women were weak, helpless creatures who should not be entrusted with the vote:

> The man over there says women need to be helped into carriages and lifted over ditches, and to have the best place everywhere. Nobody ever helps me into carriages or over puddles, or gives me the best place—and ain't I a woman? Look at my arm! I have ploughed and planted and gathered into barns, and no man could head me—and ain't I a woman? I could work as much and eat as much as a man—when I could get it—and bear the lash as well! And ain't I a woman? I have born thirteen children, and seen most of 'em sold into slavery, and when I cried out with my mother's grief, none but Jesus heard me—and ain't I a woman?[80]

The speech earned Truth a place in history. During a time when the words of black women, no matter how eloquent, were rarely recorded, this speech was written down for posterity and remembered fondly by those in attendance. Frances Dana Gage, who was presiding over the meeting, later wrote, "She [Truth] had taken us up in her strong arms and carried us safely over the slough of difficulty, turning the whole tide in our favor. I have never in my life seen anything like the magical influence that subdued the snobbish spirit of the day and turned the sneers and jeers of an excited crowd into notes of respect and admiration."[81]

The American Equal Rights Association

Following the Civil War, many of the women who had emerged as leaders of the abolition movement turned their attention wholeheartedly to women's rights, including gaining the right to vote. In 1866, the American Equal Rights Association (AERA) was formed to campaign for universal suffrage—for both men and women. The AERA included both men and women, and African American women served in prominent leadership positions, donating time and money to the cause.

Frances Harper was among the people who emerged as a leader during the three short years of the AERA's existence. Born free in the former slave state of Maryland, she had been orphaned as a child. She attended the school where her uncle taught and then earned a living as a sales clerk in a bookstore, a teacher, and a domestic servant. She also became an active volunteer for the Underground Railroad—an illegal and dangerous path to freedom for slaves that ran from the Deep South to free states in the North. Harper used her experiences to write poetry, which appeared in antislavery papers, and soon became a lecturer for antislavery societies. In contrast to Sojourner Truth, Harper was respected for the quiet dignity she brought to the cause. "She stands quietly beside her desk and speaks without notes, with gestures few and fitting," wrote an observer. "Her manner is marked with dignity and composure. She is never assuming, never theatrical."[82]

Frances Harper was a prominent leader in the American Equal Rights Association.

The Debate over Universal Suffrage

After the Civil War, the woman suffrage movement was divided over whether suffrage for women should be tied to that for black males. Although white women also struggled over this issue, African American women were in the midst of a serious philosophical debate that reached to the very heart of their identity: They were discriminated against both as blacks and as women. Frances Harper, for example, argued that black women should "let lesser question of sex go" to rally behind the Fifteenth Amendment, which would give their husbands and sons the vote. As she described it, she "would not have the black women put a single straw in the way, if only the men of the race could obtain what they wanted."[83]

Other women were committed to universal suffrage—for women as well as men—at any cost. Mary Ann Cary, who had gained stature as the editor of an abolitionist newspaper before the war, withheld support of the Fifteenth Amendment because it included the word *male*. She believed that the time was ripe for change and that women should take

Frances Harper was a prominent leader in the American Equal Rights Association.

advantage of the opportunity to protect their constitutional rights by insisting that the Fifteenth Amendment right to vote be extended to all citizens.

The debate over the issue of universal suffrage versus gradual advancements took its toll on the black organizations that had been formed to support woman suffrage. In 1869 AERA disbanded because of differences among the ideologies of its leaders. Some members of AERA (including Frances Harper) threw themselves behind the AWSA; others (including Mary Ann Cary) joined the ranks of the NWSA, which advocated more moderate approaches.

African Americans also joined state suffrage associations at a rapid rate and sometimes rose to their leadership ranks. Charlotte Remond Putnam, the daughter of a prominent abolitionist family in Salem, Massachusetts, helped found the Massachusetts Woman Suffrage Association in 1870. Josephine St. Pierre Ruffin, a Bostonian of mixed color who got her start in the woman suffrage movement with this association in 1875, "played a leading role in every movement to emancipate black women."[84]

In these and other organizations, African American women fought alongside their white sisters to gain the right to vote. They joined the lecture circuit and published articles in African American journals to gain the support of others. They

Mary Ann Cary believed that women had the same civic obligations as men, and therefore deserved equal rights.

took their argument directly to Congress. For example, Mary Ann Cary, a resident of the District of Columbia, argued before the House Judiciary Committee that she had the same obligations—including her responsibilities as a taxpayer—as her male counterparts. And black women engaged in overt acts to defend their rights as citizens. In 1871 Cary became one of the few women who successfully registered to vote. (Like so many others, she was turned away when she tried to actually cast her vote.)

Suffrage in the Post–Civil War South

In the decade following the Civil War, the South changed drastically. Many African American women—and men—believed that the process of rebuilding that followed the American Civil War, a period known as the Reconstruction, offered great promise. As the nation grappled with questions regarding how to deal with the newly emancipated slaves and what rights they should be granted, some women believed that this was their opportunity to show that they had rights as citizens as well.

Among the women who emerged as leaders in Reconstruction politics of the South were the Rollin sisters, Frances, Louisa, Kate, and Charlotte (called Lottie) of Charleston, South Carolina. These women served in leadership positions in the South Carolina Woman's Rights Association and other women's clubs. Louisa led a meeting at the state capital in 1871. Lottie, who worked for Congressman Robert Brown Elliott, pleaded the case for universal suffrage before the South Carolina House of Representatives in 1869—likely the first black woman to do so in any southern state. The next year, she argued at the South Carolina Woman's Rights Convention that suffrage was a right due to women: "We ask suffrage not as a favor, not as a privilege, but as a right based on the ground that we are human beings, and as such entitled to all human rights."[85]

This was the same argument that many whites used to demand the vote. But many African Americans took the arguments one step further. "As much as white women need the ballot, colored women need it more,"[86] Frances Harper declared at an AWSA conference. She argued that black women, particularly those in the South, were subject to the arbitrary legal authority of "ignorant and often degraded men."[87]

Black Suffragists Organize

Having traveled extensively throughout the South after the Civil War, Harper realized that black women needed the vote to defend themselves against the racism that prevailed in all aspects of their lives. This was the era of Jim Crow, where the law provided for "separate, but equal" facilities for blacks and whites. In bus stations and train depots, blacks and whites used different restrooms and water fountains. Black and white children attended separate schools, regardless of how far they had to travel. In this atmosphere, many African American women who attempted to join existing women's rights organizations were met with hostility or barred outright.

Josephine St. Pierre Ruffin, one of the first blacks to become a member of the New England Women's Club, believed that African American women needed to work together to counter racist attitudes and called on African American women to organize on their own behalf. At an 1895 convention of clubs in Boston, she declared:

For the sake of our own dignity, the dignity of our race and the future good name of our children, it is "meet, right and our bounden duty" to stand forth and declare ourselves and our principles, to teach an ignorant and suspicious world that our aims and interests are identical with those of all good, aspiring women. . . . Year after year southern women have protested against the admission of colored women into any national organization on the ground of the morality of these women, and because all refutation has only been tried by individual work, the charge has never been crushed, as it could and should have been at first. . . . It is to break this silence, not by noisy protestations of what we are not, but by a dignified showing of what we are and hope to become, that we are impelled to take this step. [88]

The National Association of Colored Women

To advance their own causes, African Americans established separate "colored" women's clubs. In addition to the rights that white women strived for, black women added the lofty goals of elevating their race and proving that they were not inferior.

The largest of these associations was the National Association of Colored Women (NACW). Formed in Washington, D.C., by Ida B. Wells-Barnett, Margaret Murray Washington, Frances Harper, Harriet Tubman, and other renowned leaders, the NACW selected Mary Church Terrell as its first president.

Terrell no doubt seemed an odd choice to some people. Many of the African American women who had emerged as

Under the leadership of Mary Church Terrell, the National Association of Colored Women represented thousands of black women's clubs from across the United States.

Women of the Suffrage Movement

"The Progress of Colored Women"

In an 1898 address before the all-white National American Women's Suffrage Association, Mary Church Terrell, cofounder and first president of the National Association of Colored Women, pointed out the differences in the experiences of white and black women, emphasized the importance of gaining access to education and employment for African Americans, and gave concrete examples of the success achieved by her "colored sisters" in the face of great obstacles. This excerpt is a page on the *Gifts of Speech: Women's Speeches from Around the World* website, hosted by Sweet Briar College.

Thus to me this semi-centennial of the National American Woman Suffrage Association is a double jubilee, rejoicing as I do, not only in the prospective enfranchisement of my sex but in the emancipation of my race....

Avocations opened and opportunities offered to their more favored sisters have been and are tonight closed and barred against them. While those of the dominant race have a variety of trades and pursuits from which they may choose, the woman through whose veins one drop of African blood is known to flow is limited to a pitiful few. So overcrowded are the avocations in which colored women may engage and so poor is the pay in consequence, that only the barest livelihood can be eked out by the rank and file. And yet, in spite of the opposition encountered, the obstacles opposed to their acquisition of knowledge and their accumulation of property, the progress made by colored women along these lines has never been surpassed by that of any people in the history of the world....

By banding themselves together in the interest of education and morality, by adopting the most practical and useful means to this end, colored women have in thirty short years become a great power for good. Through the National Association of Colored Women, which was formed by the union of two large organizations in July, 1896, and which is now the only national body among colored women, much good has been done in the past, and more will be accomplished in the future, we hope. Believing that it is only through the home that a people can become really good and truly great, the National Association of Colored Women has entered that sacred domain....

Questions affecting our legal status as a race are also constantly agitated by our women. In Louisiana and Tennessee, colored women have several times petitioned the legislatures of their respective States to repeal the obnoxious "Jim Crow Car" laws, nor will any stone be left unturned until this iniquitous and unjust enactment against respectable American citizens be forever wiped from the statutes of the South.

leaders of the woman suffrage movement were from well-to-do families in the northern states. Terrell was born to a slave mother in Tennessee. She represented what was possible for black women in post-slavery America, however. A graduate of Oberlin College, she earned acclaim as a speaker and linguist and soon became involved in all aspects of the woman suffrage movement.

Under Terrell's presidency, the NACW grew quickly to represent thousands of black women's clubs from all over the country. Like the NAWSA and other women's groups, the NACW became a vehicle to advance the cause of suffrage, publishing its own literature and hosting its own speakers bureau.

Racism in the Suffrage Movement

Racist attitudes continued to hamper the efforts of African American suffragists, however, and to keep them from the mainstream movement. Time and time again, African Americans were barred from attending or speaking at national conventions. To appease southern suffragists, many of the national organizations adopted segregation practices and discriminatory policies. At a 1900 meeting of the General Federation of Women's Clubs, Mary Church Terrell was refused permission to bring greetings on behalf of the NACW

Racism prevented Ida B. Wells-Barnett from joining white women in public protests.

after the southern clubs threatened to resign if she were allowed to do so. Even as suffrage organizations fought to generate support for a constitutional amendment that would guarantee women the right to vote, they turned away African American members. In Illinois, for example, the State Federation of Women's Clubs barred the membership of any club that admitted African Americans.

Racism was evident even among the most radical elements of the movement. In 1913 organizers of the suffrage parade had a separate section at the end of the line for African Americans in Washington and asked Ida B. Wells-Barnett, who was representing the Chicago Alpha Suffrage Club, not to march with the white delegates from Chicago.

The Paradox

By this time, African American suffragists represented a paradox. On the one hand, their numbers were useful when lobbying for the vote, and their ranks consisted of many able and educated women who made a coherent and persuasive argument for suffrage. On the other hand, they represented a liability when confronted with racist attitudes that feared giving black women any more rights. Their fight for enfranchisement threatened the woman suffrage movement from making progress. In 1917 Carrie Chapman Catt, the president of the NAWSA, reported to her board, "A serious crisis exists in the suffrage movement. . . . A considerable number of women in the South are dead set against the Federal Amendment [that would give women the vote]. The first anti-suffrage organization of importance to be affected in the South has been formed in Alabama with the slogan: 'Home Rule, States Rights, and White Supremacy.'"[89]

Some congressmen attempted to insert the words "white only" in the Anthony amendment. Others suggested an addi-tional constitutional amendment that would exclude black women. Three weeks after a suffrage amendment had been defeated in the U.S. Senate by a single vote, a young African American man wrote, "If they could get the suffrage amendment without enfranchising colored women, they would do it in a moment; all of them are mortally afraid in the South."[90]

Some suffragists tried to use racist attitudes to further their cause. Terborg-Penn writes:

> There were also strategies introduced by white women suffragists in the South to "sell" woman suffrage to Southern Congressmen and to gain their support by demonstrating that white women in the South would potentially outnumber—therefore out vote—*all* blacks in the South. Their plea for enfranchising women would be a strategy to maintain white supremacy.[91]

Barriers to the Vote

When African American women received the right to vote in the West, they took full advantage. Records indicate that African Americans were more likely than their white counterparts to exercise their new political muscle. Of the 1,373 blacks who voted in Denver, Colorado, during the 1906 election, almost half (45.2 percent) were women. However, the experiences of

African Americans had shown that a constitutional guarantee often meant little. Since the Fifteenth Amendment had granted African American males the right to vote, many states had looked for ways to disenfranchise them. They established poll taxes, designed to make voting unaffordable for poor blacks, or literacy tests, which in effect gave registrars complete discretion over who would be allowed to vote. Some states added a grandfather clause to their voting laws, dictating that only those persons whose grandfathers had voted would be allowed to vote. Since the grandfathers of the African American citizens in these Southern states had been slaves and could not vote, this clause effectively denied enfranchisement to blacks.

Another barrier to black political power was the primary election, which determined the candidates who would run in the general election. Beginning in the 1890s, Democrats in the South were able to prohibit African Americans from voting in the primary on the pretense that the Democratic Party was a private club and

Freed slaves vote in 1868. Many southern states devised poll taxes and literacy tests to keep blacks from voting.

Women of the Suffrage Movement

was thus not subject to federal laws prohibiting discrimination.

When these measures did not work, southern whites often resorted to violence to keep African Americans from voting. The Ku Klux Klan and other white supremacist groups scared African Americans away from the polls. Hundreds of blacks were killed for attempting to vote or for challenging the laws that were enacted to keep them "in their place."

When the Nineteenth Amendment was ratified in 1920, giving women the right to vote, African American women recognized that they still had a long way to go to secure political equality. They faced racism in every aspect of their lives and struggled against greater odds to gain a quality education or succeed economically. As many suffrage leaders had argued decades earlier, black women were far more in need of political power than their white sisters.

Chapter 6:
Antisuffragists

Many people assume that women were in favor of woman suffrage and men were opposed to it. In reality, just as there were many men who took up the cause of woman suffrage, there were many women who opposed it. When the pioneers of the woman suffrage movement began to spread the idea that women should have the vote, most women thought the idea ludicrous, even scandalous. As society changed, an increasing number of women began to appreciate the suffragists' argument, but female antisuffragists were vocal throughout the movement. In fact, the early twentieth century was the heyday of the antisuffrage movement, and women argued against woman suffrage even during the ratification debates of the Nineteenth Amendment in 1920.

Some women argued that politics was by definition adversarial and rough, unsuited to women's better, more genteel nature, and better left to men. Others believed that suffrage would take women's attention away from where it should be—on their homes and families—and result in the dissolution of the family and the degradation of morals. During the Progressive Era,

women similarly argued that voting would add to the list of demands on women's time and take attention away from the reform movement. They also believed that their strength lay in remaining a nonpartisan and independent force. In the South, particularly in states in which African Americans were a majority, women opposed universal suffrage because they feared giving additional political power to blacks.

Of course, people were also opposed to suffrage for political and economic reasons. In particular, suffragists met with considerable opposition from the powerful liquor interest, which believed that women would use the vote to outlaw the sale of alcohol. Big business, too, joined the so-called antis in their fight against suffrage because corporate leaders believed women would vote for reforms that would cost them money.

When Antis Were the Majority

When Elizabeth Cady Stanton added the vote to the list of demands at the Seneca Falls Convention in 1848, even her staunchest allies worried that they would be ridiculed or labeled as extremists.

Newspaper accounts of early woman suffrage meetings demonstrated the widespread opinion that woman suffrage was a ludicrous—even appalling—idea. One editorial after another argued that politics was "dirty business" better left to men. Women and men alike believed that they had different spheres and that a woman's place was in the home. An editorial in the *Mechanics Advocate* in Albany, New York, declared:

A poster urges voters to reject suffrage. Many women believed that involvement in politics would interfere with their role as homemakers.

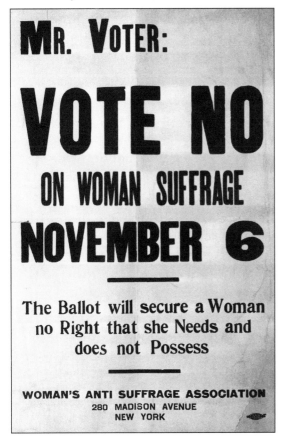

We are sorry to see that the women in several parts of this State are holding what they call "Women's Rights Conventions" and setting forth a formidable list of those Rights in a parody upon the Declaration of Independence.... Now it requires no argument to prove that this is all wrong. Every truehearted female will instantly feel that this is unwomanly. ... [Woman suffrage] would produce no positive good, that would not be outweighed tenfold by positive evil.[92]

Most women agreed. Historian Doris Weatherford writes:

Indeed, most women had to be talked into their own liberation, slowly persuaded that they were worthy of the same rights that their husbands, brothers, and sons took for granted. The tendency to invest in the status quo [existing state of affairs] is in fact so strong that for decades, organizations dedicated to maintaining the bonds that held women down were, in fact, headed by women.[93]

The Early Argument

The antisuffrage arguments used by men and women often differed. Many men argued that women lacked the intellect for political involvement, but women tended to discount this argument, focusing instead on their role as housewives and mothers. Put simply, a woman's place was in the home, and women should let their husbands worry about politics and government. In 1878, at the first congressional session that heard testimony regarding woman suffrage, Madeleine Vinton Dahlgren, a wealthy widow, testified before Congress in opposition, arguing, "When women ask for a distinct political life, a separate vote, they forget or willingly ignore the higher law, whose logic may be condensed: Marriage is a sacred unity. . . . Each family is represented through its head." [94]

The antisuffrage argument also focused on women's genteel nature and often portrayed the suffragists as domineering, masculine figures who wanted nothing to do with home life. Put simply, women and men were biologically different and were suited for different spheres. During debate over the Fifteenth Amendment, one senator mused, "It seems to me as if the God of our race has stamped upon [the women of

---

Women Don't Want the Vote

One of the main arguments of the women who led the antisuffrage movement was that most women simply did not want enfranchisement. The following excerpt from a letter to the editor of the *New York Times* was written in 1873 and signed "A Woman." It is reprinted in *Forward into Light,* edited by Madeleine Meyers.

I believe, from all I have ever been able to ascertain, that for every one woman who desires to vote, there are ten [at least] who do not wish to do so. And are we, the majority of educated women in this country, to have political duties thrust upon us, which we not only do not desire, but utterly abhor! In our hatred of publicity, in our desire to keep utterly aloof from a matter which is so distasteful to us, we have said too little, have kept silence too long, until the strong-minded party think we care nothing about it. Could I speak with a thousand tongues, it would be to give a hundred thousand reasons why we should not vote. We can use our influence in our homes, a woman's proper sphere, and who can tell how much we do use it now! It is all we want. Let almost any woman who has a family to care for speak, and say how much time she has to devote to the study of political questions, and to the duties which are incumbent upon voters. . . . To the women of our land who yet love their own womanly sphere, I say, Keep silence in public when you can; but work, work at home in your own dominion, that we may be saved from this fate.

Women of the Suffrage Movement

Ellen Ewing Sherman submitted a petition against woman suffrage to the U.S. Senate in 1872.

America] a milder, gentler nature, which not only makes them shrink from, but disqualifies them for the turmoil and battle of public life."[95]

Some women found it difficult to reconcile their opinion that women should not participate in politics with their need to convince others of this opinion. Female antisuffragists occasionally voiced their resolve to "leav[e] the political end entirely to men"[96] and hired male agents to lobby on their behalf. In 1882 two women appeared at a legislative hearing to argue against giving women the right to vote in municipal elections in Massachusetts. They "preserved their modesty"[97] by presenting a written statement instead of verbal testimony.

Yet, even the earliest antisuffragists found it necessary to get the work done themselves by appearing before congressional committees or other political forums to testify on their own behalf. Antisuffragists engaged in other lobbying tactics as well. As early as 1872, Ellen Ewing Sherman, wife of famous Civil War general William Tecumseh Sherman, and Madeleine Vinton Dahlgren, wife of famous Civil War admiral John Dahlgren, were instrumental in obtaining one thousand signatures for a petition to the U.S. Senate against woman suffrage.

The Antis Organize

As the suffragists made strides in swaying public opinion, the antisuffragists began to organize in opposition. In 1882 antisuffragists came together as the Massachusetts Association Opposed to the Further Extension of Suffrage to Women following an unsuccessful bid for woman suffrage in that state. By 1900 antisuffragists had formed associations in New York, Illinois, California, South Dakota, Washington, and Oregon; a decade later, antisuffrage associations existed in at least twenty states. In 1911 antisuffragists formed the National Association Opposed to Woman Suffrage (NAOWS), headquartered in New York.

A group of men reads information posted in front of the headquarters of the National Association Opposed to Woman Suffrage. Such organizations were founded, staffed, and led by women.

These antisuffrage organizations were founded, staffed, and led by women. The leaders were women of irreproachable social position and from well-established families with strong political connections— connections that they used to their advantage. Later antisuffragists often had close ties to business interests. In 1910 two of the national women's antisuffrage organizations were led by women who were married to directors of railroads. The asso-

ciations drew almost exclusively from the middle and upper classes of society—those who believed they would lose influence and social standing by allowing lower classes of women to vote.

From the beginning, the antisuffrage associations supported like-minded women across the nation in states where there was woman suffrage legislation pending or a referendum scheduled. In the 1880s, for example, the Boston Committee of Remonstrants sent funds and antisuffrage literature to their sisters in Oregon during that state's referendum campaign.

Explaining Their Rationale

The antisuffragists wrote pamphlets, posters, and articles—antisuffrage organizations often set as their primary goal publishing and circulating information against woman suffrage and appealing to the "large majority of thinking women"[98] opposed to female voting rights. Antis found it far easier than did suffragists to find newspapers and magazines willing to publish their treatises. As suffrage meetings became more common, the popular press abounded with editorials and articles expounding why women should not have the vote. And an increasing number of these articles were written by women.

Women also published journals dedicated to opposing woman enfranchisement. The *Remonstrance,* the earliest publication dedicated to the antisuffrage cause, began publication in 1890 and would continue to publish articles in opposition to

---

The Antisuffrage Sentiment

A late as the 1910s, many people believed that granting women the right to vote would undermine the ability of women to take care of their homes and children. In a 1913 speech at a meeting held by the New York State Association Opposed to Woman Suffrage, the women in the audience applauded Everett P. Wheeler's speech, in which he combined a tribute to motherhood with a dire warning about a future in which women are allowed to vote. This excerpt is taken from *Forward into Light,* edited by Madeleine Meyers.

It is the status of the women in America under our existing sytem that more than anything else has made this country what it is. . . . It is upon mothers that the whole burden of future America rests, more than upon Legislatures.

Nothing shows more clearly the failure of the suffragists, to realize the facts of the case than their favorite argument, that it is no burden to spend a few minutes putting a piece of paper in a box. If this is all they want let them set up boxes of their own and have a play election once a year.

But, in fact, the agitation they promote . . . means they want a full share in civil government. If this object was attained it needs no prophet to predict that it would destroy the peace of families and that in the end it would destroy the country and the race.

---

woman suffrage until 1920. When the NAOWS was formed, it launched its own publication, the *Woman's Protest*. In addition to arguments against granting women the right to vote, the antisuffrage journals provided readers with reports about woman suffrage defeats in various states, as well as examples of instances in which enfranchised women in western states had failed to use their votes to better society.

Women wrote almost all of the articles in the antisuffrage periodicals. They also explained why they were opposed to the vote in longer, more elaborate dissertations. Perhaps the most influential of the antisuffrage books was *Woman and the Republic* by Helen Johnson. Johnson and her husband, Rossiter, were both active members of the antisuffrage movement in New York. In *Woman and the Republic,* Helen Johnson responded to the arguments put forth by suffragists, using statistics and anecdotes to demonstrate that women did not need the vote to improve their legal and economic position. She also argued that a woman's role in the separate, domestic sphere was

A Puck *magazine cartoon caricatures suffragists as men signing the Declaration of Independence. Antisuffragists circulated their message in a number of publications.*

Women of the Suffrage Movement

critical to maintaining the family ties so important for an orderly society.

When *Woman and the Republic* hit the newsstands in 1897, it was met with praise from across the nation. "If the woman suffrage movement is ever to be finally defeated, it will be by women themselves," wrote one reviewer, "and by arguments and considerations like those so ably stated in this remarkable book." [99]

Antisuffrage; Pro-Rights

Like Johnson, many of the women who were active in the antisuffrage movement believed that the vote was not necessary for making other gains. In fact, many antisuffragists were ardent defenders of women's rights. "Give woman everything she wants," declared Jeanette L. Gilder in an 1894 pamphlet, "but not the ballot. Open every field of learning, every avenue of industry to her, but keep her out of politics." [100]

Annie Nathan Meyer, who played a key role in the establishment of Barnard College, was an associate editor of the *Woman's Patriot*. She argued that women's rights had been gained not because of the work of woman suffragists, but in spite of it. In one article, Meyer wrote, "The women who really blazed the paths of education and reform in this country were either outspoken antisuffragists or at best lukewarm suffragists who were too busy doing their work to bother about imaginary wrongs." [101]

During the Progressive Era, the antisuffragists crystallized their rationale: Granting women the right to vote, they said, would undermine their ability to effect reform. By aligning themselves with a political party, they would lose the advantage of being nonpartisan, politically independent entities. Josephine Jewell (Mrs. Arthur) Dodge, a prominent society figure who served as the president of the NAOWS for most of its existence, stated in 1916:

> We believe that women according to their leisure, opportunities, and experience should take part increasingly in civic and municipal affairs as they always have done in charitable, philanthropic and educational activities, and we believe that this can best be done without the ballot by women, as a non-partisan body of disinterested workers. [102]

One antisuffragist wrote of her civic responsibilities: "Just as fervently as the Suffragists, do the Anti-Suffragists desire to be citizens, and intend to be citizens. . . . We Anti-Suffragists feel that we not only can be and are citizens without the ballot, but that we shall remain better citizens without it than with it." [103] To defend their claims, the antisuffragists pointed to female social workers, reformers, and activists who maintained that they would not have accomplished what they did if they had had the right to vote—that it was their political neutrality that led others to see their arguments as valid or worthy of attention.

Some antisuffragists focused on the fact that the franchise would add to women's burdens and would take attention away from their other civic responsibilities. A group of New Hampshire women, claiming to represent "women of every station in life," testified in 1913 that "with the demands of society, calls of charity, the church, and philanthropy constantly increasing, we feel that to add the distracting forces of political campaigns would wreck our constitutions and destroy our homes."[104] To defend this point of view, antisuffrage organizations cited statistical and anecdotal evidence that illustrated the decline of women's civic and reform associations in suffrage states.

Opposition from the Liquor Interests

The women who led the antisuffrage movement had powerful allies. Among the most vehement opponents of woman suffrage were brewers, liquor wholesalers, and saloon keepers—a coalition that some suffragists referred to as "the Hidden Enemy."[105] State campaigns were often thwarted by the liquor interest. During the 1896 suffrage campaign in California, for example, San Francisco's liquor companies sent a letter to saloon keepers, hotel proprietors, druggists, and grocers throughout the state urging them to vote against giving women the right to vote. "It is to your interest and ours to vote against this amendment. We request and urge you to vote and work against it and do all you can to defeat it. See your neighbor in the same line of business as yourself, and have him be with you in this matter."[106] In Nebraska, an organizer working on behalf of the brewers admitted that the liquor interest had defeated woman suffrage in 1911 "at tremendous expense and by active work of the brewers being on the job all the time and not leaving it to somebody else."[107]

The brewing interest worked mostly behind the scenes, however, providing financial aid and advice to woman antisuffrage organizations. Carrie Chapman Catt complained that "a trail led from the women's organizations into the liquor camp and it was traveled by the men the women antis employed. . . . These men were observed in counsel with the liquor political manager too often to doubt that they laid their respective plans before each other so far as cooperation could be of advantage."[108]

In a 1914 letter marked "confidential" to a Milwaukee brewer, Catt's charge was confirmed:

In regard to the matter of woman suffrage, we are trying to keep from having any connection with it whatever. We are, however, in a position to establish channels of communication with the leaders of the anti-suffrage movement for our friend in any state where suffrage is an issue. . . . I consider it most dangerous to have the [liquor] retailers identified or active in any way in this fight, as it will be used against us everywhere. [109]

Antis Benefit from Big Business

Railroad, oil, general manufacturing, and other big business also opposed allowing women to vote. They worried that women would use the vote to improve the conditions of working women (and children), ushering in reforms that would cost them money. Maud Wood Park, who headed the NWSA's Congressional Committee for four years, wrote that many "were fearful that tariff schedules might be reduced or railroad regulation extended if women had a chance to vote." [110]

Businesses lobbied tenaciously in places where suffrage was up for legislative action or referendum. An appeal urging Nebraskans to vote against that state's

Railroad and other big business campaigned against suffrage. A 1913 poster proclaims the antisuffrage views of the Canadian Pacific Railway.

1914 woman suffrage referendum, for example, carried the signatures of nine railroad and municipal transit executives, seven bankers, and a host of other businessmen. Business lobbies also sent sample articles to newspapers with the request that they be published as editorials under the editor's byline.

As with the liquor interest, much of the work went on covertly. The business lobby often worked through antisuffrage organizations, coordinating campaigns and offering advice on strategy. The greatest influence of business, however, came in the form of money. Compared to the limited funds available to suffrage organizers, the antis had ample assets from which to draw. Reports from three antisuffrage organizations in Massachusetts that had been active in defeating that state's 1915 campaign revealed that the majority of their contributions had come from individuals and four-fifths from men, totaling $31,695. "What sort of man can afford to sign a check for $235 with which to fight the enfranchisement of women?" asked an editorial in the *Woman's Journal*. "The powerful directors of the moneyed section of Boston." [111]

Politics at the Hands of the Electorate

Among the most vehement arguments women made against woman suffrage was that it would allow an increased number of "undesirables" to vote. "The primary objection to woman suffrage is that it would add an enormous army of unqualified voters to the huge mass of them that vote now," [112] summed up one 1906 editorial.

In fact, it was this concern that drew many women to the movement. One suffrage worker described a prominent woman who "preferred not to claim the right [of suffrage] for herself, lest its concession entail the enfranchisement of ignorant and irresponsible women." [113] Another antisuffragist in Boston warned her colleagues, "If the great mass of ignorant women's votes are added to the great mass of ignorant men's votes there will be constant demands for work, money, bread, leisure, in short 'all kinds of laws to favor all kinds of persons.'" [114]

The issues varied according to where people lived. Northeasterners worried about the immigrant vote; in the West, it was "prostitutes, frontier riff-raff, and political machines" [115] who were viewed as the enemy. But nowhere was the argument that woman suffrage would upset the natural order of things more prevalent than in the South. Southerners feared that woman suffrage would eliminate the poll tax and other voting restrictions that had effectively denied African Americans the vote, and they were adamant about keeping elections as a states' rights issue.

During the bitter battle at the ratification convention in Tennessee, Carrie

An Antisuffrage Petition to Congress

❦

By 1916 almost all of the major suffrage organizations were united behind the goal of a constitutional amendment. When New York adopted woman suffrage in 1917 and President Woodrow Wilson changed his position to support an amendment in 1918, the political balance began to shift in favor of the vote for women. There was still strong opposition to enfranchising women, however, as illustrated by this petition from the Women Voters Anti-Suffrage Party of New York at the beginning of U. S. involvement in World War I. This introduction and the petition are from the website of the U.S. National Archives and Record Administration at www.archives.gov.

Whereas, This country is now engaged in the greatest war in history, and Whereas, The advocates of the Federal Amendment, though advocating it as a war measure, announce, through their president, Mrs. Catt, that its passage 'means a simultaneous campaign in 48 States. It demands organization in every precinct; activity, agitation, education in every corner. Nothing less than this nation-wide, vigilant, unceasing campaign will win ratification,' therefore be it

Resolved, That our country in its hour of peril should be spared the harassing of its public men and the distracting of its people from work for the war, and further

Resolved, That the United States Senate be respectfully urged to pass no measure involving such a radical change in our government while the attention of the patriotic portion of the American people is concentrated on the all-important task of winning the war, and during the absence of over a million men abroad.

Chapman Catt warned suffrage leaders, "The antisuffragists will flood Tennessee with the most outrageous literature it has ever been your lot to read. It will be extremely harmful, and the 'nigger question' will be put forth in ways to arouse the greatest possible prejudice."[116] Antisuffrage propaganda capitalized on southern racist attitudes and fears. One opponent of suffrage warned, "the passage of the Nineteenth Amendment would embolden both the negro [sic] woman and the negro man to give us even greater trouble than they are doing now."[117]

Southern antisuffragists attacked those who would vote for woman suffrage as traitors to their region. Mildred Rutherford, the president of the Georgia United Daughters of the Confederacy, told the Georgia legislature in 1914: "Woman's suffrage comes from the North and West and from women who do not believe in state's rights and who wish to see negro women using the ballot. I do not believe the state of Georgia has sunk so low that her good men can not legislate for the women."[118]

Even women who had once fought for state legislation that would grant them the right to vote argued against a constitutional amendment that would undermine states' rights. Laura Clay of Kentucky and Kate Gordon of Louisiana, for example, both ended long careers of suffrage work on the state and national levels to oppose the ratification of the Nineteenth Amendment.

The Contributions of Female Antisuffragists

In the end, the women who argued against suffrage brought increased credibility to antisuffrage arguments. They also added a new argument: that women did not want the vote. Antisuffragists pointed to the throng of women who fought the vote and argued that the suffragists were but a vocal minority. By this argument, enfranchising women was undemocratic; it would not only cave to the will of the minority but would require women to do something they did not want to do. In an 1876 letter to the editor of the New York Times, "A

Woman" writes: "I believe, from all I have ever been able to ascertain, that for every one woman who desires to vote, there are ten [at least] who do not wish to do so. And are we, the majority of educated women in this country, to have political duties thrust upon us, which we not only do not desire, but utterly abhor!"[119]

Thirty years later, antisuffragists continued to argue that suffragists were in the minority. A 1906 article in Life magazine declares, "There is nothing the average American woman wants that the average American man will not give her if he can get it. He can give her the voting privilege, and he will give it to her when she wants it. But, as yet, she does not want it and he has no mind to force it upon her."[120]

Woman suffragists had been agitating for the right to vote for over half a century. Although they had made modest gains, the record shows that they still had not convinced the majority of the electorate nor the majority of the men who represented them in Congress. Even more troubling, however, was the fact that the suffrage movement still could not claim the allegiance of all women. To the bitter end of the struggle, there remained vocal, intelligent, and well-connected women who simply believed that woman suffrage was a bad idea.

Chapter 7:
The Mighty Pen: Women Writers and Orators

❧

Throughout the struggle for suffrage, women had to defend their opinions and convince others to agree. As suffragists sought to expand membership in suffrage organizations and to persuade men to vote for their cause, the written word became an important weapon in the suffragists' arsenal. Of particular importance were the writers who worked behind the scenes, carefully crafting the suffrage message. In broadsides, pamphlets, newspaper editorials, magazine articles, and suffrage newsletters, the suffragists argued their case.

The pro-suffrage argument changed over time to adapt to changes taking place in society. The early suffragists claimed the vote as a natural right as citizens of a democracy. Later women argued that, with the vote, women could play a key role in municipal politics and much-needed reforms. By the early twentieth century, some suffragists accommodated the anti-suffrage claim that women should focus on their responsibilities in the domestic sphere by arguing that only through obtaining the vote could women fulfill their responsibilities as wives and mothers.

Finally, there were women who contributed to the cause by recording the arguments, actions, and inactions of the movement and its leaders. The majority of the women who wrote these accounts were not academically trained as historians or journalists. For the most part, they were veterans of the suffrage movement who, Ellen Carol DuBois writes, "believed that the preservation of history would contribute to 'the cause.'"[121]

Finding Their Voice

In the early days of the suffrage movement, the woman suffragists resigned themselves to publishing their argument wherever the editors would accept their articles. The press in general was unsupportive of women's rights at best—most articles that were published in mainstream newspapers and magazines portrayed both women and attempts to gain rights as silly, foolhardy, or downright dangerous. Women often found abolitionist newspapers, such as William

Lloyd Garrison's the *Liberator*, to have the most receptive audience.

A few women published their own journals, touching on themes considered liberal for their day. These included the *Lily*, a journal "Devoted to the Interests of Women" that was edited by Amelia Bloomer, who made pantslike bloomers popular dress for liberated women. The *Woman's Advocate*, a Philadelphia paper that was owned, edited, and printed by a coalition of women, focused on gaining economic rights for women. For a brief time, there was also the *Una*, which was published by Paulina Wright Davis, a wealthy Rhode Island socialite who was instrumental in the first women's rights conferences. The February 1853 inaugural issue of the *Una* announced: "Our purpose is to discuss the rights, duties, sphere, and destiny of women fully and fearlessly."[122] Davis was devastated when the *Una* failed; she wrote, "we have come to feel, mortifying as is the truth, that woman's freedom must first be proclaimed by man, that her own hand will never strike the blow or her heart pulsate to freedom's note till her oppressor wakens her from the dreamless sleep of her present life."[123]

One of the more popular writers for these papers was Frances Dana Gage. An early suffrage organizer and lecturer, under the pen name "Aunt Fanny," Gage won over many skeptics with a combination of tact and satire. She wrote myriad

Paulina Wright Davis published the short-lived journal Una *in 1853.*

articles for the *Lily* and other feminist papers that interspersed practical advice for housewives with witty reflections on women's position in society. In "The Perplexed Housekeeper," for example, a poem published in 1867, she talked of her ability to earn a living prior to marriage as compared with a wife's duty "doing the work of six; *For the sake of being supported!*"[124]

The *Revolution*

While these feminist publications included women's rights among their issues, none had gaining rights as its sole focus. Recognizing that there was a void in the pro-suffrage literature, Susan B. Anthony, Elizabeth Cady Stanton, and Parker Pillsbury (who left his job as an editor at the *Standard*) launched the *Revolution,* a weekly newspaper published under the motto "Principle, Not Policy; Justice, Not Favors; Men Their Rights and Nothing More; Women Their Rights and Nothing Less."[125] First issued in January 1868, the paper only lasted for three years, but its influence went far beyond its humble beginnings. Historians Flexner and Fitzpatrick explain:

The weekly sixteen-page paper, smaller than today's tabloids, made a contribution to the women's cause out of all proportion to either its size, brief lifespan, or modest circulation. . . . [T]he *Revolution* did more than just carry news, or set a new standard of professionalism for papers edited by and for women. It gave their movement a forum, focus, and direction. It pointed, it led, and it fought, with vigor and vehemence. Its editorials and leading articles inveighed against

The *Revolution*

T he following excerpt from the editorial of the first issue of the *Revolution,* January 8, 1868, is taken from *Forward into Light,* edited by Madeleine Meyers.

A NEW paper is the promise of a new thought; of something better or different, at least, from what has gone before.

With the highest idea of the dignity and power of the press, this journal is to represent no party, sect, or organization, but individual opinion; editors and correspondents alike, all writing from their own stand point, and over their own names. The enfranchisement of woman is one of the leading ideas that calls this

journal into existence. Seeing, in its realization, the many necessary changes in our modes of life, we think "THE REVOLUTION" a fitting name for a paper that will advocate so radical a reform as this involves in our political, religious and social world.

With both man and woman in the editorial department, we shall not have masculine and feminine ideas alone, but united thought on all questions of national and individual interest. . . .

Determined to do our part in pushing on the car of progress we begin . . . a new life work, hoping the world will be the better for the birth of "THE REVOLUTION."

discrimination in employment and pay, the inequities of divorce procedure, the derogatory concept of women fostered by established religion, as well as the injustice of the Fourteenth and Fifteenth Amendments. It exhorted women to equip themselves to earn their own livelihood, to practice bodily hygiene in the matter of fresh air, dress, and exercise, and it campaigned for the vote as basic to any kind of equality.[126]

The *Revolution* told of women in all walks of life—from factory workers to farmers, from typesetters to tailoresses, from sailors to inventors. The editors also wrote and reprinted articles on issues not often discussed by genteel society, such as birth control, prostitution, and cooperative housekeeping. One historian calls the paper "the most daring feminist paper that had yet—and perhaps has ever—appeared. In its pages, the editors . . . tried to convey a complex sense of women's oppression and a rich vision of their emancipation."[127] Women's rights and woman suffrage, of course, were recurring themes.

The *Woman's Journal*

As the *Revolution* aired the views of the NWSA, the AWSA published its own paper: the *Woman's Journal*. Beginning with its first issue a year after the *Revolution*, the *Woman's Journal* was edited by Lucy Stone, her husband, Henry Blackwell, and Mary Livermore.

Livermore seems a natural choice as editor of the *Woman's Journal*. She was no stranger to the woman suffrage movement and had organized the first suffrage convention in Chicago in 1869. She also had ample experience as an editor, first of a reform newspaper called the *New Covenant*, and later of the *Agitator*, a newspaper she founded to advocate woman suffrage. Livermore used the *Agitator* to demand

Mary Livermore was editor of the Woman's Journal, *a publication designed to circulate the views of the American Woman Suffrage Association.*

Women of the Suffrage Movement

political equality for women. Each issue contained a variety of articles written by Livermore and others promoting suffrage as both a "natural right" that society owed to women and a way to allow an under-utilized group to contribute its considerable skills toward the creation of a better nation. Like the *Revolution,* the *Agitator* focused on the many achievements women were making in various professions, but the latter made a more moderate appeal to middle- and upper-class women.

In 1870 Livermore merged the *Agitator* with the *Woman's Journal* and moved to Boston to serve as its editor. "Devoted to the Interests of Woman, to her Education, Industrial, Legal and Political Equality and especially her right to Suffrage,"[128] the *Woman's Journal* was far less radical than the *Revolution.* Flexner and Fitzpatrick write that this paper "drew around it as contributors and readers the rapidly growing numbers of women emerging into the greater social freedom and multiple activity of the '70s—club women, professionals, and writers."[129]

Pamphlets, Posters, Propaganda, and the Press

The suffragists spread the word not only through journals and books, but also through pamphlets and broadsides, often distributed at their speaking engagements. From the beginning, these proved to be valuable propaganda, reaching audiences far beyond those in attendance. In the South, pamphlets were often the only source of information about women's rights or suffrage.

In the last decade of the nineteenth century, women also made greater use of humorous postcards and cartoons to bring attention to their cause. Children were often the subject of suffrage postcards, which were frequently sold to raise money for the cause. One popular postcard shows a little boy trying to kiss a girl who, holding him at arms length, says, "Suffrage First!"[130] Another postcard shows a prominent gentleman at a street-corner suffrage speech who suddenly realizes—to his horror—that the speaker is his daughter. The caption reads, "And he thought she was just a little girl!"[131]

The mainstream press avoided women cartoonists, so the first female cartoonists resigned themselves to working for publications such as the *Woman's Journal.* They used their skill to counteract the depiction of suffragists as masculine, unfriendly people. Women cartoonists tended to show suffragists in traditional female roles, even as they emphasized the need for suffrage. Over time, however, pro-suffrage cartoons took on a more militant tone. Later cartoons, such as the ones by Nina Allender that were featured on the covers of the *Suffragist,* cast a negative light on politicians. Men who opposed woman suffrage in general were shown as hard-hearted, dim-witted, or corrupt.

Suffrage Humor

As the woman suffrage movement matured, it began to mimic the tactics of the male antisuffragists, such as poking humor and ridicule at the other side, as Jim Zwick explains in "Political Cartoons and Cartoonists" (available at www.boondocks net.com), from which this excerpt is taken.

The woman suffrage movement was a subject for both satire and support by male cartoonists and a source of inspiration for female cartoonists who broke into the profession at the end of the nineteenth century and first decades of the twentieth. Political cartoons about the suffrage movement depicted specific events but also presented images of male and female roles in society; their dress, demeanor, and characteristics; and the consequences of women's increased political activity. Many of the anti-suffrage cartoons expressed male fears of losing power to women and included images like hen-pecked husbands, "mere men" or crazed or dominant women that are still repeated today.

Political cartoons about the suffrage movement drawn by women were usually published in specialized magazines like the *Woman's Journal, The Suffragist,* and *Woman Voter* and did not receive as much circulation as cartoons drawn by men for the mainstream press. They were very important, however, in presenting an alternative view of the movement. Women cartoonists presented their own interpretations of the issues, and their portrayals of women were more favorable than those produced by some male cartoonists.

Suffragists also tried to reach new audiences by flooding the media with press releases. In the 1890s, the NAWSA created committees in forty-one states that aimed to get weekly press releases in local newspapers. More than 25,000 press releases were mailed in 1897; five years later, this number had increased to 175,000. The association also began publishing the *National Suffrage Bulletin* (later called *Progress*) to track the progress of local and state legislative efforts.

Campaigning in California in the early 1900s, woman suffragists began to use more sophisticated communications mechanisms, including billboards and even electric signs. They printed about 4 million pamphlets and leaflets in Italian, German, and French as well as English. Woman suffragists also placed agents at the polls, equipped with money for telegrams to identify questionable or fraudulent activities.

By the 1910s, the NAWSA press department played a key role. Through it, the NAWSA researched women's voting habits to allay fears and correct misinformation. The NAWSA also collected data from county clerks in states where women voted, including facts on women in office, laws relating to women and suffrage, and other related topics. Of primary importance was the relationship that NAWSA's press office formed with the editors of mainstream newspapers and journals. The result of the press office's unwavering attention was that many editors "who were wavering have been persuaded to come out definitely in favor; this has been especially noticeable in the South." [132]

Suffrage historian Helena Woods (left) visits cartoonist Nina Allender. Allender's cartoons portrayed politicians as hard-hearted, dim-witted, and corrupt.

African American Writers

Denied a role as organizers in the major suffrage organizations, African Americans often made the most advantage of the written word. Adella Hunt Logan and Nannie Helen Burroughs were among the African American women who wrote articles in defense of woman suffrage. Logan, a native of Georgia who had moved to Alabama to join the Tuskegee Institute faculty, picked up on earlier arguments that black women, as victims of racism *and* sexism, needed the ballot even

Nannie Helen Burroughs wrote many articles in support of woman suffrage.

more than white women to protect their rights. Among the media for her arguments was the *Crisis,* the magazine of the National Association for the Advancement of Colored People (NAACP), an organization formed in 1909 to protest the mistreatment of blacks in the United States and rectify the problems caused by racism. Burroughs, who had achieved a national reputation as the founder of the National Training School for Women and Girls, also published woman suffrage articles in the *Crisis* and other black publications.

Ida B. Wells-Barnett had proven that writing could be a powerful tool. Born a slave in a small town in Mississippi just six months before the Emancipation Proclamation, her parents died when she was just fourteen, leaving her to raise four younger brothers and sisters. Wells-Barnett worked for several years as a teacher and began writing for the new African American newsletters that were blossoming throughout the South. In 1890 she became the editor of the *Memphis Free Speech.* She used this platform to lament the plight of black people. When she criticized black schools as inferior, she lost her job as a teacher. But she had found a new calling as a writer.

Wells-Barnett took up a career as a journalist, focusing particular attention on the lynchings that were taking place in the South. Historians Eleanor Flexner and Ellen Fitzpatrick write that she "launched a veritable one-woman campaign against lynchings through the columns of other papers, on the lecture platform, and by helping to found colored women's clubs in Boston, New York, Chicago, and the Middle West." [133]

When Wells-Barnett was driven out of the South because of her crusade against lynching, she settled in Chicago. There, she founded the first black woman's suffrage association, the Alpha Suffrage Club. Rosalyn Terborg-Penn writes that Wells-Barnett was "virtually unique in her time as a woman who espoused a radical philosophy for racial and gender equality." [134]

Speaking Out for Suffrage

In addition to writing, woman suffrage advocates spread their ideas in lectures, debates, and rallies. Often, these speeches played a key role in state suffrage campaigns; orators traveled from one town to another and often gave literally hundreds of speeches. Olympia Brown, a Massachusetts Unitarian reverend, traveled to Kansas in 1876 to campaign on behalf of woman suffrage. There, Brown organized, advertised, and delivered an estimated three hundred speeches. She proved her oratory skills in a public debate with an antisuffrage judge—the last such debate the antisuffragist camp in Kansas allowed. The *Kansas State Journal* reported that when the audience was asked to stand if they agreed with Brown, "nearly every

Betty Graham (left) and Olympia Brown pose as the youngest and oldest suffragettes at a convention. The suffrage movement spanned seventy-two years.

man and woman in the house rose simultaneously." [135]

Effective orators also made an impact speaking at national and state conventions for women's rights. After meeting Susan B. Anthony at an 1888 convention, Anna

Howard Shaw, for example, devoted herself to woman suffrage. Although she is often criticized for her lack of organizing skills as the president of NAWSA, she generated enthusiasm within the movement with her stirring and passionate speeches. On behalf of the NAWSA, she campaigned in every state where a suffrage measure was under consideration. Before, during, and after her ten-year stint as president of the NAWSA, Shaw continued to gain renown as an orator. In a 1910 speech, she reminded the audience of the gains that had been won and encouraged them to see the movement through to the end: "The real reformer does not judge of the reform from the day or of an hour, but traces its progress from the beginning, and no human being with the eye of faith can fail to see traversing the whole progress of our movement a divinity shaping our ends . . . and that divinity is the gospel of democracy." [136]

Progressivism and the Feminist Argument

Like the woman suffrage movement itself, the arguments that were printed in defense of giving women the vote varied greatly and changed over time. In 1894 Elizabeth Cady Stanton, who wrote volumes on the woman suffrage movement, wrote a pamphlet entitled *Suffrage, a Natural Right,* in which she expounded upon the age-old argument that, as citizens, women were entitled to the right to vote.

Over time, this argument gave way to the argument that giving women the right to vote was politically expedient. Lucy Stone, for example, wrote articles in the *Woman's Journal* explaining that women could use the franchise to protect themselves better than men were protecting them. Similarly, Catharine Waugh McCulloch, a lawyer, emphasized the need for women to protect themselves against imperfect laws written by men. Women journalists—a new and growing breed—supported such arguments in their reports on the conditions of women in all walks of life.

As working women became a higher percentage of the population and a more dominant force within the movement, many writers began to connect them to the suffrage argument. Florence Kelley, for example, a lawyer who devoted herself to working with the poor, wrote many articles explaining that working women needed the vote to protect themselves against the special hazards that women in factories faced. Eleanor Kirk, an aspiring journalist, wrote a series of articles called "Heart Aching Facts" for the *Revolution,* describing in a factual, detailed manner the working conditions under which women toiled in New York. Flexner and Fitzpatrick describe a seminal 1894 woman suffrage pamphlet entitled *"Common Sense" Applied to Woman Suffrage,* in which Mary Putnam Jacobi, a New York physician, wrote that "so-called 'women's work' was now so frequently and evidently non-domestic . . . [that it] could no longer be considered something exclusively done in the personal service of father or husband,"[137] thus removing any basis for a man's control of his wife's property and earnings, or claim that he could represent her politically. In other writings, Jacobi demonstrated how changes that were taking place in society made granting women the vote inevitable. The educational advancement of women, she argued, "and the new activities into which they have been led by it—in the work of charities, in the professions, and in the direction of public education—naturally and logically tend toward the same result, their political equality."[138]

Perhaps the most influential of these women was Charlotte Perkins Gilman, a lecturer, poet, novelist, and journalist. In *Women and Economics,* published in 1898, Gilman discussed the evolution of the sexes and argued that most human ills resulted from women's dependence on men. Only by becoming economically independent could balance be restored, and suffrage was key to this independence.

Jane Addams and the Progressives

Suffragists also reached an ever wider audience, moving beyond proponents of the movement into the mainstream press. In the first decade of the twentieth century,

well over a hundred articles on the issue appeared in popular American magazines. Magazines and journals regularly published news stories about the activities of the suffragists, as well as arguments used for and against granting women the right to vote. Articles also were written about the experience of western states where the vote had been won, describing both the experience of these first women voters and whether or how they were affecting political decision making. Increasingly often, the authors of the articles pointed to suffrage as "a natural evolution which can no more be stopped than the tides of the sea."[139]

The argument put forth by the suffragists was influenced by the Progressive movement spreading across the nation during this time. Rather than arguing against the idea of separate spheres—women working in the home, men in politics—the suffragists often argued that industrialization and urbanization made it necessary for women to engage in politics in order to protect their homes and children. One widely used suffrage poster stated: "Women are by nature and training housekeepers. Let them help in the city housekeeping. They will introduce an occasional spring cleaning."[140]

One of the most widely read and reproduced woman suffrage articles of this time was written by author, speaker, and social reformer Jane Addams for the January 1910 issue of the *Ladies' Home*

Journal, a magazine that was at the time on record in opposition to woman suffrage. During her lifetime, Addams wrote more than five hundred articles, twelve books, and lectured prolifically, but the article "Why Women Should Vote" gave a new twist to an old argument. Addams, a beloved Progressive figure, stated strongly that women could not fulfill their traditional functions without the power afforded by the vote. "If women would effectively continue their old avocations they must take part in the slow upbuilding of that code of legislation which is alone sufficient to protect the home from the dangers incident to modern life," she wrote. The essay ended:

> If woman would fulfill her traditional responsibility to her own children; if she would educate and protect from danger factory children who must find recreation on the street; if she would bring the cultural forces to bear upon our materialistic civilization; and if she would do it all with the dignity and directness fitting one who carries on her immemorial duties, then she must bring herself to the use of the ballot— that latest implement for self government. May we not fairly say that American women need this implement in order to preserve the home?[141]

In a book written during the same period, Addams used the same argument to demonstrate how giving women a role to play in politics would help rid government of corruption and clean up the cities: "May we not say," she asked, "that city housekeeping has failed partly because women, the traditional housekeepers, have not been consulted as to its multiform activities?"[142]

Making History

Well before the Nineteenth Amendment gave women the right to vote in 1920, woman suffragists were determined that theirs was a story to be told—and that they were the ones to tell it. In fact, Elizabeth Cady Stanton proposed writing a book on the history of women's yearnings for rights as early as the 1840s. In the early 1870s she teamed up with Susan B. Anthony and Matilda Joslyn Gage to write a book on the history of woman suffrage. She rejected criticism that theirs would be a biased account by saying that "a history written by its actors get[s] nearer the soul of the subject."[143] What began as a single manuscript evolved into a six-volume compendium published over forty-seven years and designed to establish the movement in the historical record.

Stanton, Anthony, and Gage were not professional writers, but they collected and saved as many materials as they could, resulting, as historians Flexner and

Will Women Change Politics?

❦

Following the ratification of the Nineteenth Amendment, much speculation concerned the effect of woman suffrage on politics and society. The following editorial from the August 29, 1920, issue of the *New York Times* brings up questions about the future and captures the struggle for woman suffrage. This editorial is excerpted from "The Passage of the 19th Amendment, 1919–1920," available from the *Modern History Sourcebook* website at www.fordham.edu.

Women in fighting for the vote have shown a passion of earnestness, a persistence, and above all a command of both tactics and strategy, which have amazed our master politicians. A new force has invaded public life. . . . What is to be the upshot?

It is doubtless true that women will divide much as men have done among the several parties. There will be no solid 'woman vote.' Having individual opinions and preferences, they will be individually swayed by them in respect to any given political issue or personality. But this is only half of the story. Even the democratic franchise cannot quite unsex either men or women. Hitherto the distinctively feminine instincts and aspirations have centered in winning the right of suffrage; but now that it is won, a vast, united force has been let loose. That political issues and leaders should continue to be merely man-made is inconceivable.

It is a fair guess, and indeed a fact already exemplified, that one distinctive interest of the woman politician will be in what is called welfare legislation—the regulation of the conditions of life and of industry with reference to the health and vigor of the nation, for the present and especially for future generations. Such issues should rouse all the powers of sisterly and motherly instinct. . . .

Women are . . . developing a flexibility of mind and a capacity for compromise that make political discussion a thing very different from what it has been. Again, in the current campaign both parties are appealing to the feminine abhorrence of bloodshed, and especially to the desire to protect brothers and sons; but, while one party declares that the League of Nations will end all wars, the other, with equal assurance, declares that it will ceaselessly embroil us. . . . By degrees the bickerings of politics as practiced by men are developing a really vital view of the situation. Women who are fit to be mothers of the nation know that there is no sovereign remedy against death in any form, and that the one sure way to make life honorably safe is to face its responsibilities with a clear mind and a high heart. True citizenship means service and sacrifice, the giving as well as the taking.

Fitzpatrick note, in "an immense grab-bag of source material."[144] The newspaper clippings, speeches, and letters that they accumulated contributed greatly to the ability of later historians to access primary source materials.

The last three volumes were written in large part by Ida Husted Harper, a professional writer who served as the suffrage movement's most prolific publicist. She wrote volumes about and for the suffrage

Ida Husted Harper wrote prolifically about the achievements women made toward suffrage and equality.

movement and contributed greatly to the "canonization" of Susan B. Anthony. In keeping with the NAWSA's new emphasis on respectability, she composed an article in 1903 that contradicted the stereotype many people had of women suffragists in general, and Anthony in particular, as antithetical to domesticity. Entitled "Miss Anthony at Home," the article portrayed Anthony as "domestic in every fiber of her body."[145] After Anthony's death, Harper collected over a thousand editorials that eulogized Anthony. She also completed a three-volume biography shortly after Anthony's death.

Harper also wrote prodigiously about the achievements women had made toward suffrage and toward equality. In a *North American Review* article, for example, Harper traced the history of the franchise in America and described how conditions had changed as a result of hard-won legal reforms and increased educational opportunities afforded to women.

Historical Bias

The history written by Stanton, Harper, and others is admittedly biased. Other accounts, such as Doris Stevens's account of the suffragettes in *Jailed for Freedom,* are similarly one-sided and somewhat self-aggrandizing. They were nonetheless important to the movement, both as symbols of what women wanted to achieve and the obstacles they faced in reaching

Women of the Suffrage Movement

their goals. Sara Hunter Graham writes about the impact of this history on the suffrage movement:

> History of this sort was important to the suffrage movement in several ways. First, NAWSA leaders drew from women's, and particularly suffrage, history a tradition of leadership handed down from pioneer suffragists and women's rights activists, canonized in the *History of Woman Suffrage* and hagiographic accounts of that movement's early workers and imbued with the legacy of a century of heroic struggle. As the lineal successors of Anthony, Stanton, and Stone, twentieth-century leaders found legitimation for their position through the celebration of, and association with, what might be called the "founding mothers" of their organization. [146]

It is in large part from these historians and others that we know the details of the woman suffrage struggle, of the women at the forefront of the movement and those who worked behind the scenes, of their triumphs and frustrations, of the tireless devotion of so many to win the vote.

Notes

Introduction: The Long Struggle for Suffrage

1. Quoted in Marjorie Spruill Wheeler, ed., *One Woman, One Vote: Rediscovering the Woman Suffrage Movement*. Troutdale, OR: NewSage Press, 1995, p. 25.
2. Quoted in Eleanor Flexner and Ellen Fitzpatrick, *Century of Struggle: The Woman's Rights Movement in the United States*. Cambridge, MA: Belknap Press, 1996, p. xxxiii.

Chapter 1: Pioneers for Woman Suffrage

3. Quoted in Elizabeth Cady Stanton, Susan B. Anthony, and Matilda Joslyn Gage, *History of Woman Suffrage*, vol. 1. Rochester: 1881, p. 61.
4. Quoted in Eleanor Flexner, *Century of Struggle: The Woman's Rights Movement in the United States*. Cambridge, MA: Belknap Press, 1975, p. 48.
5. Quoted in Miriam Gurko, *The Ladies of Seneca Falls: The Birth of the Woman's Rights Movement*. New York: MacMillan, 1974, p. 40.

6. Gurko, *The Ladies of Seneca Falls*, p. 35.
7. Quoted in Gurko, *The Ladies of Seneca Falls*, p. 55.
8. Elizabeth Cady Stanton, *Eighty Years and More: Reminiscences, 1815–1897*. New York: Schocken Books, 1975, pp. 147–48.
9. Stanton, *Eighty Years and More*, p. 148.
10. Quoted in Mari Jo Buhle and Paul Buhle, eds., *The Concise History of Woman Suffrage: Selections from the Classic Work of Stanton, Anthony, Gage, Harper*. Urbana: University of Illinois Press, 1978, p. 91.
11. Quoted in Buhle and Buhle, *The Concise History of Woman Suffrage*, p. 94.
12. Quoted in Flexner, *Century of Struggle*, p. 76.
13. Quoted in Gurko, *The Ladies of Seneca Falls*, p. 100.
14. Quoted in Wheeler, p. 43.
15. Quoted in Gurko, *The Ladies of Seneca Falls*, p. 104.
16. Quoted in Gurko, *The Ladies of Seneca Falls*, p. 103.

17. Quoted in Ellen Carol DuBois, *Feminism and Suffrage: The Emergence of an Independent Women's Movement in America, 1848–1869.* Ithaca, NY: Cornell University Press, 1999, p. 48.

18. Quoted in Buhle and Buhle, *The Concise History of Woman Suffrage,* p. 99.

19. Quoted in Wheeler, *One Woman, One Vote,* p. 62.

20. Quoted in Stanton, Anthony, and Gage, *The History of the Woman Suffrage Movement,* p. 634.

21. DuBois, *Feminism and Suffrage,* p. 41.

22. Quoted in Flexner and Fitzpatrick, *Century of Struggle,* p. 81.

23. DuBois, *Feminism and Suffrage,* pp. 23–24.

Chapter 2: National Organizers and the Political Struggle

24. Quoted in Wheeler, *One Woman, One Vote,* pp. 62–63.

25. Quoted in Wheeler, *One Woman, One Vote,* p. 46.

26. Quoted in DuBois, *Feminism and Suffrage,* p. 61.

27. Quoted in Wheeler, *One Woman, One Vote,* p. 71.

28. Quoted in Wheeler, *One Woman, One Vote,* p. 71.

29. Quoted in Doris Stevens, *Jailed for Freedom: American Women Win the Vote.* Troutdale, OR: NewSage Press, 1995, p. 14.

30. Quoted in Flexner and Fitzpatrick, *Century of Struggle,* p. 165.

31. Quoted in Flexner and Fitzpatrick, *Century of Struggle,* p. 166.

32. Flexner and Fitzpatrick, *Century of Struggle,* p. 175.

33. Quoted in Flexner and Fitzpatrick, *Century of Struggle,* p. 176.

34. Quoted in Wheeler, *One Woman, One Vote,* p. 63.

35. Quoted in Wheeler, *One Woman, One Vote,* p. 298.

36. Quoted in Flexner and Fitzpatrick, *Century of Struggle,* p. 273.

37. Quoted in Wheeler, *One Woman, One Vote,* p. 308.

38. Quoted in Doris Weatherford, *A History of the American Suffragist Movement.* Santa Barbara, CA: ABC-CLIO, 1998, p. 228.

39. Quoted in Weatherford, *A History of the American Suffragist Movement,* p. 221.

Chapter 3: Grassroots Organizers: Working at the Local Level

40. Quoted in DuBois, *Feminism and Suffrage,* p. 85.

41. DuBois, *Feminism and Suffrage,* p. 85.

42. Quoted in Weatherford, *A History of the American Suffragist Movement*, p. 94.

43. Flexner and Fitzpatrick, *Century of Struggle*, p. 155.

44. Quoted in Allen Kent Powell, ed., "Emmeline Wells," *Utah History Encyclopedia*, University of Utah Press. www.media.utah.edu.

45. Flexner and Fitzpatrick, *Century of Struggle*, p. 152.

46. Quoted in Weatherford, *A History of the American Suffragist Movement*, p. 185.

47. Quoted in Flexner and Fitzpatrick, *Century of Struggle*, p. 229.

48. Quoted in Wheeler, *One Woman One Vote*, p. 225.

49. Quoted in Wheeler, *One Woman, One Vote*, p. 163.

50. Quoted in Flexner and Fitzpatrick, *Century of Struggle*, p. 216.

51. Quoted in Wheeler, *One Woman, One Vote*, pp. 236–37.

52. Marjorie Spruill Wheeler, *New Women of the New South: The Leaders of the Woman Suffrage Movement in the Southern States.* New York: Oxford University Press, 1993, p. xvii.

53. Quoted in Wheeler, *New Women of the New South*, p. 134.

54. Quoted in Flexner and Fitzpatrick, *Century of Struggle*, pp. 312–13.

55. Quoted in Wheeler, *One Woman, One Vote*, p. 336.

56. Quoted in Wheeler, *One Woman, One Vote*, p. 345.

57. Quoted in Weatherford, *A History of the American Suffragist Movement*, p. 243.

58. Quoted in Wheeler, *One Woman, One Vote*, p. 347.

Chapter 4: Militant Suffragists

59. DuBois, *Feminism and Suffrage*, p. 49.

60. Quoted in Buhle and Buhle, *The Concise History of Woman Suffrage*, p. 285.

61. Quoted in Weatherford, *A History of the American Suffragist Movement*, pp. 113–14.

62. Quoted in Flexner, *Century of Struggle*, p. 169.

63. Quoted in Wheeler, *One Woman, One Vote*, p. 34.

64. Quoted in Wheeler, *One Woman, One Vote*, p. 236.

65. Weatherford, *A History of the American Suffragist Movement*, p. 198.

66. Quoted in Wheeler, *One Woman, One Vote*, p. 281.

67. Quoted in Stevens, *Jailed for Freedom*, p. 33.

68. Quoted in Stevens, *Jailed for Freedom*, p. 27.

69. Quoted in Wheeler, *One Woman, One Vote*, p. 240.

70. Quoted in Wheeler, *One Woman, One Vote*, p. 240.

71. Quoted in Stevens, *Jailed for Freedom*, p. 18.

72. Quoted in Stevens, *Jailed for Freedom*, p. 36.

73. Quoted in Weatherford, *A History of the American Suffragist Movement*, p. 198.

74. Quoted in Stevens, *Jailed for Freedom*, p. 40.

75. Stevens, *Jailed for Freedom*, p. 63.

76. Stevens, *Jailed for Freedom*, p. 81.

77. Quoted in Madeleine Meyers, ed., *Forward into Light: The Struggle for Woman's Suffrage*. Carlisle, MA: Discovery Enterprises, 1994, p. 58.

Chapter 5: African American Women in the Suffrage Movement

78. Quoted in Wheeler, *One Woman, One Vote*, p. 138.

79. Quoted in Flexner and Fitzpatrick, *Century of Struggle*, p. 41.

80. Quoted in Flexner and Fitzpatrick, *Century of Struggle*, p. 85.

81. Quoted in Flexner and Fitzpatrick, *Century of Struggle*, pp. 85–86.

82. Quoted in Flexner and Fitzpatrick, *Century of Struggle*, p. 91.

83. Quoted in Flexner and Fitzpatrick, *Century of Struggle*, p. 138.

84. Quoted in Wheeler, *One Woman, One Vote*, p. 140.

85. Quoted in Wheeler, *One Woman, One Vote*, pp. 140–41.

86. Quoted in Wheeler, *One Woman, One Vote*, p. 142.

87. Quoted in Wheeler, *One Woman, One Vote*, p. 142.

88. Quoted in Flexner and Fitzpatrick, *Century of Struggle*, p. 182.

89. Quoted in Flexner and Fitzpatrick, *Century of Struggle*, p. 267.

90. Quoted in Flexner and Fitzpatrick, *Century of Struggle*, p. 297.

91. Quoted in Stevens, *Jailed for Freedom*, p. 196.

Chapter 6: Antisuffragists

92. Quoted in Meyers, *Forward into Light*, pp. 8–9.

93. Weatherford, *A History of the American Suffragist Movement*, p. 1.

94. Quoted in Weatherford, *A History of the American Suffragist Movement*, p. 130.

95. Quoted in Flexner and Fitzpatrick, *Century of Struggle*, p. 142.

96. Quoted in Wheeler, *One Woman, One Vote*, p. 206.

97. Flexner and Fitzpatrick, *Century of Struggle*, p. 287.

98. University of Texas, *The Handbook of Texas Online*. www.tsha.utexas.edu.

99. Quoted in Wheeler, *One Woman, One Vote*, p. 206.

100. Quoted in Wheeler, *One Woman, One Vote,* p. 210.

101. Quoted in Wheeler, *One Woman, One Vote,* p. 216.

102. Quoted in Wheeler, *One Woman, One Vote,* p. 209.

103. Quoted in Wheeler, *One Woman, One Vote,* p. 212.

104. Quoted in Aileen S. Kraditor, *The Ideas of the Woman Suffrage Movement, 1890–1920.* New York: W.W. Norton, 1981, p. 28.

105. Flexner and Fitzpatrick, *Century of Struggle,* p. 216.

106. Quoted in Flexner and Fitzpatrick, *Century of Struggle,* p. 216.

107. Quoted in Flexner and Fitzpatrick, *Century of Struggle,* p. 216.

108. Quoted in Flexner and Fitzpatrick, *Century of Struggle,* p. 289.

109. Quoted in Flexner and Fitzpatrick, *Century of Struggle,* p. 289.

110. Quoted in Flexner and Fitzpatrick, *Century of Struggle,* p. 293.

111. Quoted in Flexner and Fitzpatrick, *Century of Struggle,* p. 292.

112. Quoted in Jone Johnson Lewis, "Women's History," The History Net, 1999. http://womenshistory. about.com.

113. Quoted in Ellen Carol DuBois, *Woman Suffrage and Women's Rights.* New York: New York University Press, 1998, p. 181.

114. Quoted in Kraditor, *The Ideas of the Woman Suffrage Movement,* p. 31.

115. Kraditor, *The Ideas of the Woman Suffrage Movement,* p. 30.

116. Quoted in Wheeler, *One Woman, One Vote,* p. 344.

117. Quoted in Wheeler, *One Woman, One Vote,* p. 344.

118. Quoted in Wheeler, *New Women of the New South,* p. 25.

119. Quoted in Meyers, *Forward into Light,* p. 34.

120. Quoted in Lewis "Women's History."

Chapter 7: The Mighty Pen: Women Writers and Orators

121. DuBois, *Woman Suffrage and Women's Rights,* p. 210.

122. Quoted in Weatherford, *A History of the American Suffragist Movement,* p. 65.

123. Quoted in Buhle and Buhle, *The Concise History of Woman Suffrage,* p. 13.

124. Quoted in Women and Social Movements in the United States, December 2002. http://womhist. binghamton.edu.

125. Quoted in Weatherford, *A History of the American Suffragist Movement,* p. 105.

126. Flexner and Fitzpatrick, *Century of Struggle,* pp. 144–45.

127. DuBois, *Feminism and Suffrage,* p. 104.

128. Quoted in Buhle and Buhle, *The Concise History of Woman Suffrage,* p. 22.

129. Flexner and Fitzpatrick, *Century of Struggle,* p. 146.

130. Quoted in Stevens, *Jailed for Freedom,* p. 29.

131. Quoted in Stevens, *Jailed for Freedom,* p. 29.

132. Quoted in Weatherford, *A History of the American Suffragist Movement,* p. 216.

133. Flexner and Fitzpatrick, *Century of Struggle,* p. 181.

134. Quoted in Stevens, *Jailed for Freedom,* p. 196.

135. Quoted in Weatherford, *A History of the American Suffragist Movement,* p. 96.

136. Quoted in Wheeler, *One Woman, One Vote,* p. 167.

137. Flexner and Fitzpatrick, *Century of Struggle,* p. 223.

138. Quoted in DuBois, *Woman Suffrage and Women's Rights,* p. 180.

139. Quoted in Wheeler, *One Woman, One Vote,* p. 187.

140. Quoted in Wheeler, *One Woman, One Vote,* p. 181.

141. Quoted in Wheeler, *One Woman, One Vote,* p. 201.

142. Quoted in Kraditor, *The Ideas of the Woman Suffrage Movement,* p. 70.

143. Quoted in DuBois, *Woman Suffrage and Women's Rights,* p. 213.

144. Flexner and Fitzpatrick, *Century of Struggle,* p. 338.

145. Quoted in Wheeler, *One Woman, One Vote,* p. 172.

146. Quoted in Wheeler, *One Woman, One Vote,* p. 108.

Important Dates in the Suffrage Movement

1776

In a letter to her husband, future president John Adams, Abigail Adams warns him to "Remember the Ladies" in the nation's new constitution.

1833

The first female antislavery society is formed in Philadelphia. Early suffragists built on their experiences and the skills they acquired as activists in many antislavery societies.

1836

Sarah Grimké begins her speaking career as an abolitionist and women's rights advocate.

1839

Mississippi passes the first Married Woman's Property Act, giving women the right to own property.

1840

Lucretia Mort and Elizabeth Cady Stanton meet at the World Anti-Slavery Convention in London, England.

1848

The Seneca Falls Convention convenes in New York on July 19–20; at the end of the two-day event, conference participants publish the Declaration of Sentiments, based on the Declaration of Independence; for the first time in the United States, women publicly demand the right to vote.

1850

The first National Women's Rights Convention is held in Worcester, Massachusetts. National conventions would be held annually for the next ten years (except 1857).

1851

Ex-slave Sojourner Truth delivers her "Ain't I a Woman?" speech before a captivated audience at a women's rights convention in Akron, Ohio.

1855

Lucy Stone marries Henry Blackwell, who shares her passion for woman suffrage and the abolition of slavery; the couple eliminate the vow of obedience from the wedding ceremony and include a protest against unfair marriage laws.

1866

The American Equal Rights Association is formed to work on behalf of universal suffrage; Lucretia Mott presides over its inaugural meeting.

1867

Kansas holds a referendum to decide the issue of woman suffrage; prominent suffragists, including Lucy Stone, Henry Blackwell, Clarina Nichols, and others, travel to Kansas to support their cause.

1868

The Fourteenth Amendment is ratified July 28, extending to all citizens the protections of the Constitution against unjust state laws; in this amendment, the Constitution first defines *citizens* and *voters* as "male."

1869

The suffrage movement splits into the National Woman Suffrage Association, which opposes passage of the Fifteenth Amendment and is led by Elizabeth Cady Stanton and Susan B. Anthony, and the American Woman Suffrage Association, which supports the amendment and is led by Lucy

Stone and Julia Ward Howe; Wyoming becomes the first U.S. territory to allow women to vote in all elections.

1870

The territory of Utah enfranchises women; the Fifteenth Amendment is ratified March 30, declaring that no citizen may be denied the right to vote on account of "race, color, or previous condition of servitude," but gender or sex is not included on the list of protected categories.

1870–1875

Women attempt to use the Fourteenth and Fifteenth Amendments as grounds for their right to cast a ballot; singly and in groups they head to the polls; several sue election officials for denying them the right to vote.

1872

Many women across the country, including Susan B. Anthony, attempt to vote in the presidential election; Anthony is among those arrested and fined, generating national publicity. She steadfastly refuses to pay the fine.

1874

In *Minor v. Happersett,* the Supreme Court rules that the Fifteenth Amendment does not grant women the right to vote; the Woman's Christian Temperance Union is formed; the leaders of the alcohol prohibition movement, convinced that they will need the power of the vote to succeed, join the woman suffrage movement.

1875

Women in Michigan and Minnesota are granted the right to vote in school elections.

1878

An amendment to the Constitution that would give women the right to vote is introduced in Congress but fails to pass by the required two-thirds senate majority; supporters pledge to reintroduce the proposal (which soon became known as the "Anthony amendment") every year until it is passed; the wording is unchanged through 1919, when the amendment finally passes both houses.

1882

The Massachusetts Association Opposed to the Further Extension of Suffrage to Women is formed, becoming the first antisuffrage organization.

1890

The National Woman Suffrage Association and the American Woman Suffrage Association merge to become the National American Woman Suffrage Association; Wyoming enters the Union with its woman suffrage provisions intact, becoming the first state to grant woman suffrage.

1896

The National Association of Colored Women is formed.

1900

Carrie Chapman Catt takes over presidency of the National American Woman Suffrage Association (NAWSA).

1910

Washington State grants woman suffrage.

1911

The National Association Opposed to Woman Suffrage is formed; California grants woman suffrage.

1912

Alice Paul chairs the Congressional Committee of the NAWSA in Washington, D.C.; Oregon, Arizona, and Kansas grant woman suffrage.

1913

The Congressional Union (which became the National Woman's Party in 1916) is formed; under Alice Paul, the group used radical tactics to gain publicity for the cause of woman suffrage; a suffrage parade is held in Washington, D.C., during the inauguration of President Woodrow Wilson; Illinois grants women a new form of partial suffrage by allowing them to vote only in presidential elections.

1916

NAWSA president Carrie Chapman Cart unveils her "winning plan" for suffrage, which requires a coordination of activities by state suffrage associations; Jeannette Rankin of Montana is elected to the U.S. House of Representatives, becoming the first woman in Congress.

1917

Suffragettes picket the White House for ten months; hundreds are arrested and 168 jailed; behind bars they draw sympathy and attention by going on hunger strikes; eight more states grant women partial or full suffrage.

1919

President Woodrow Wilson calls a special session of Congress to reconsider the Anthony amendment, which is finally passed by the Senate June 4, 1920; on August 18 the state of Tennessee becomes the thirty-sixth state to ratify the Nineteenth Amendment to the Constitution, and the amendment is adopted August 26; it states: "The right of citizens of the United States to vote shall not be denied or abridged by the United States or by any state on account of sex."

For Further Reading

❧

Books

Marlene Targ Brill, *Let Women Vote!* Brookfield, CT: Millbrook Press, 1996. This book for high school students traces the development of the woman suffrage movement and its leaders.

Kathryn Cullen-DuPont, *Elizabeth Cady Stanton and Women's Liberty.* New York: Facts On File, 1992. This biography uses excerpts from the speeches and writings of Elizabeth Cady Stanton to provide a vivid portrait of the life and work of one of the premier figures in the women's suffrage movement.

Kristina Dumbeck, *Leaders of Women's Suffrage.* San Diego, CA: Lucent Books. This book in Lucent's History Makers series gives brief biographies of the women who led the fight for the right to vote.

Jeanne Gehret, *Susan B. Anthony: And Justice for All.* Fairport, NY: Verbal Images Press, 1994. A readable, lively biography of Anthony and her work in the woman suffrage, abolitionist, and temperance movements. Archival photographs and reproductions enliven the narrative.

Miles Harvey, *Cornerstones of Freedom: Women's Voting Rights.* New York: Childrens Press, 1996. An easy-to-read text of the struggle for the right to vote, enhanced by photographs and reproductions.

Judy Monroe, *The Nineteenth Amendment: Women's Right to Vote.* Springfield, NJ: Enslow Publishers, 1998. This easy-to-read account of the struggle women undertook to gain the right to vote through a constitutional amendment begins with an account of the 1848 Seneca Falls Convention.

Angelina Osborne, *Abigail Adams: Women's Rights Advocate.* New York: Chelsea House, 1989. This portrait of one of America's earliest advocates for women's rights focuses on the influences on Abigail Adams and on the influences she had on her husband and other powerful people around her.

Hertha E. Pauli, *Her Name Was Sojourner Truth.* New York: Avon, 1976. This popular biography includes imagined conversations with this African American who championed abolition and woman suffrage causes.

Betsy Covington Smith, *Women Win the Vote*. Englewood Cliffs, NJ: Silver Burdett Press, 1989. This illustrated account of the road to women's suffrage highlights the tireless work that was undertaken by the women who led the struggle.

Websites

Anthony Center for Women's Leadership (www.rochester.edu.) Dedicated to keeping the fight for equality alive, the Anthony Center's website includes a brief history of the movement and links to other useful information.

Library of Congress, National American Woman Suffrage Association (http://memory.loc.gov.) The Library of Congress website provides a brief history of the NAWSA as well as several important documents, images, and links to brief biographical sketches of the NAWSA's leaders and other sites.

National Women's History Project (www.nwhp.org.) The mission of the National Women's History Project is to recognize and celebrate the diverse and historic accomplishments of women by providing information and educational materials and programs. The website includes biographies of famous women (including suffragists) and links to woman suffrage websites.

Public Broadcasting System (www.pbs.org.) This website includes "The History of the Suffrage Movement" by Marjorie Spruill Wheeler, an easy-to-read overview of the woman suffrage movement written by a historian who has written several books on the topic.

U.S. National Records and Archives Administration (www.archives.gov.) This archive of hundreds of documents in their original form and entirety includes several that relate to the fight for woman suffrage.

Women and Social Movements in the United States, 1775–2000 (http://womhist.binghamton.edu.) A project of the Center for the Historical Study of Women and Gender at the State University of New York at Binghamton, the website currently contains forty-two "mini-monographs," each of which poses an interpretive question and provides a collection of documents that address the question. Altogether, the site includes over nine hundred documents, nearly four hundred images, and 350 links to other websites and is an excellent resource for primary materials on woman suffrage and women's rights.

Works Consulted

Books

Mari Jo Buhle and Paul Buhle, eds., *The Concise History of Woman Suffrage: Selection from the Classic Work of Stanton, Anthony, Gage, and Harper.* Urbana: University of Illinois Press, 1978. These selections from the six-volume History of Woman Suffrage series offer readers a wealth of primary source material, categorized by date and subject matter.

Ellen Carol DuBois, *Feminism and Suffrage: The Emergence of an Independent Women's Movement in America, 1848–1869.* Ithaca, NY: Cornell University Press, 1999. A study of the origins of the nineteenth-century American suffrage movement, which DuBois calls the first feminist movement in the United States.

————, *Woman Suffrage and Women's Rights.* New York: New York University Press, 1998. This series of articles on woman suffrage traces the trajectory of the suffrage story against the backdrop of changing attitudes to politics, citizenship, and gender.

Eleanor Flexner, *Century of Struggle: The Woman's Rights Movement in the United States.* Cambridge, MA: Belknap Press, 1975. Written in the 1950s, this historical account of the woman's rights movement that begins with the moment women set foot on American soil discusses the women who fought for suffrage, the prejudices they encountered, and the fears they overcame.

Eleanor Flexner and Ellen Fitzpatrick, *Century of Struggle: The Woman's Rights Movement in the United States.* Cambridge, MA: Belknap Press, 1996. This revised version of the book adds contemporary perspective to Flexner's classic account of the women's rights movement.

Miriam Gurko, *The Ladies of Seneca Falls: The Birth of the Woman's Rights Movement.* New York: MacMillan, 1974. A highly readable and detailed account of the women's rights movement and those who paved the way for suffrage and equality.

Aileen S. Kraditor, *The Ideas of the Woman Suffrage Movement, 1890–1920.* New York: W.W. Norton, 1981. This book discusses the various ideas and ideologies that moved millions of women to demand the right to vote.

Madeleine Meyers, ed., *Forward into Light: The Struggle for Woman's Suffrage*. Carlisle, MA: Discovery Enterprises, 1994. This collection of journals, news clips, poems, songs, essays, and political cartoons from the woman suffrage movement tells the story of the movement and the women who led it through their writing, speeches, and actions.

Nancy M. Neuman, ed., *A Voice of Our Own: Leading American Women Celebrate the Right to Vote*. San Francisco: Jossey-Bass, 1996. This collection of twenty-nine essays written by prominent American women—politicians, journalists, academics, activists, and other professionals—chronicles the experiences of those involved in the women's suffrage movement.

Donald W. Rogers, ed., *Voting and the Spirit of American Democracy: Essays on the History of Voting and Voting Rights in America*. Urbana: University of Illinois Press, 1992. Written by leading historians and political scientists, these essays tracing the history of American voting from the colonial period to the present include discussions of women's suffrage.

Elizabeth Cady Stanton, *Eighty Years and More: Reminiscences, 1815–1897*. New York: Schocken Books, 1975. Reprinted from an 1898 edition, this book describes the struggle of American women toward equality from the vantage point of one of its greatest advocates.

Elizabeth Cady Stanton, Susan B. Anthony, and Matilda Joslyn Gage, *History of Woman Suffrage*. Vols. 1–3. Rochester: n.p., 1881. This detailed insiders' view of the women's suffrage movement provides a wealth of newspaper clippings, speeches, letters, and other primary materials collected by the authors.

Doris Stevens, *Jailed for Freedom: American Women Win the Vote*. Troutdale, OR: NewSage Press, 1995. This account of the woman suffrage movement, told by a participant in 1920, unfolds the remarkable story of Alice Paul and other militant suffragists.

Geoffrey C. Ward and Ken Burns, *Not for Ourselves Alone: The Story of Elizabeth Cady Stanton and Susan B. Anthony*. New York: Alfred A. Knopf, 1999. This companion to the PBS special focuses on the friendship and partnership of two of the greatest leaders of the women's suffrage movement.

Doris Weatherford, *A History of the American Suffragist Movement*. Santa Barbara, CA: ABC-CLIO, 1998. A lively and readable history of the women's suffrage movement in America, from its roots in colonial America to its ties to other nineteenth-century reform movements to the passage of the Nineteenth Amendment.

Marjorie Spruill Wheeler, *New Women of the New South: The Leaders of the Woman Suffrage Movement in the Southern States.* New York: Oxford University Press, 1993. The story of the women who led the fight for suffrage in the South, the region where suffragists had the hardest fight and the least success.

———, ed., *One Woman, One Vote: Rediscovering the Woman Suffrage Movement.* Troutdale, OR: NewSage Press, 1995. This companion to the PE special of the same name provides a comprehensive look at the women's suffrage movement, with chapters devoted to specific groups and periods within the movement.

Internet Sources

Allen Kent Powell, ed., *Utah History Encyclopedia.* University of Utah Press. www.media.utah.edu.

E. Susan Barber and Barbara Orbach Natanson, "One Hundred Years Toward Suffrage." http://lcweb2.loc.gov.

Frances Dana Gage, "The Perplexed Housekeeper," Women and Social Movements. www.womhist.bing hamton.edu.

History Channel, "Woman's Suffrage." www.historychannel.com.

Jim Zwick, "Political Cartoons and Cartoonists." www.boondocksnet.com.

Jone Johnson Lewis, "Women's History," The History Net, 1999. http://womens history.about.com.

Kris Kobach, "Rethinking Article V: Term Limits and the Seventeenth and Nineteenth Amendments," *Yale Law Journal.* www.law.cornell.edu.

"The Passage of the 19th Amendment, 1919–1920," *Modern History Sourcebook.* www.fordham.edu.

Susan B. Anthony Center for Women's Leadership, University of Rochester, "Biographies of Suffragists," June 13, 2002. www.rochester.edu.

Mary Church Terrell, "The Progress of Colored Women," *Gifts of Speech: Women's Speeches from Around the World.* http://gas.sbc.edu.

University of Texas, *The Handbook of Texas Online.* www.tsha.utexas.edu.

Index

see also women's suffrage movement

Washington, Margaret Murray, 72
WCTU. *See* Woman's Christian
  Temperance Union
Weatherford, Doris, 56, 79
Weil, Gertrude, 50
Weld, Angelina Grimké, 53
see also Grimké, Angelina
Wells, Emmeline B., 38
Wells-Barnett, Ida B., 72, 75, 98–99
Wheeler, Everett P., 83
Wheeler, Marjorie Spruill, 18, 46–47
"Why Women Should Vote" (article), 102
Willard, Frances, 28–29
Williams, Sarah, 36
Wilson, Woodrow, 32, 34, 60, 62–64, 89
Winning Plan, 31
Woman and the Republic (Helen Johnson),
  84–85
Woman's Advocate (newspaper), 92
Woman's Bible (Elizabeth Cady Stanton), 14
Woman's Christian Temperance Union
  (WCTU), 28–29, 46
Woman's Journal (magazine), 26, 88, 94–96,
  100

Woman's Patriot (magazine), 85
Woman's Political Union (WPU), 55
Woman's Protest (periodical), 84
Woman Voter (magazine), 96
Women and Economics (Gilman), 101
women's rights
  limitations of, 18
  states pass bills in favor of, 21, 24,
    36–37
  support of, by antisuffragists, 85–86
Women's Social and Political Union
  (WSPU), 57
Women Voters Anti-Suffrage Party, 89
Woodhull and Claflin's Weekly (periodical),
  52
Woodhull, Victoria, 52
Woodward, Charlotte, 15–16
World Anti-Slavery Convention, 12, 14
WPU. *See* Woman's Political Union
Wright, Martha C., 13
WSPU. *See* Women's Social and Political
  Union

Yale Law Journal, 42

Zwick, Jim, 96

Picture Credits

Cover photo: © Hulton/Archive by
    Getty Images
© Bettmann/CORBIS, 7, 9, 74, 79
© CORBIS, 45, 69, 76, 82, 84, 92, 94,
    97, 104
© Hulton/Archive by Getty Images,
    37, 52, 59, 62, 87
Library of Congress, 11, 12, 20, 23, 27,
    29, 30, 33, 38, 39, 49, 54, 58, 66, 72

National Archives of Canada, 70
Schomburg Center for Research in
    Black Culture, 98
© Smithsonian American Art Museum,
    Washington, D.C./Art Resource,
    NY, 81
© Lee Snider; Lee Snider/CORBIS, 16
© Underwood & Underwood/
    CORBIS, 99

About the Author

Lydia Bjornlund is a private consultant and freelance writer, focusing primarily on issues related to civic education, government, and training. She is the author of books and training manuals, as well as numerous magazine and newsletter articles. This is her fifth book for Lucent Books.

Ms. Bjornlund holds a master of education from Harvard University and a bachelor of arts from Williams College, where she majored in American studies. She lives in Oakton, Virginia, with her husband, Gerry Hoetmer, and their twins, Jake and Sophia.